MUSEUM ADVENTURES

ABOUT THE BOOK

MUSEUM ADVENTURES is a book that travels.

Visiting museums all over the United States, Herbert and Marjorie Katz enable the reader to move backward in time and forward in space.

In a single volume, the authors have created a mosaic of human achievement. Here one painting can be the stepping-stone to Impressionism, one coat of mail the spur to a whole age of chivalry, one bone a key to the mystery of evolution.

"History," "Art," "Science" and "Some Very Special Places" form the main divisions of the book. More than a hundred photographs highlight the text.

The museums chosen are sometimes large, sometimes small; the exhibits within well known or obscure.

But in each case a new horizon is discovered. A new gateway into the arena of man's adventure opens.

MUSEUM

An Introduction

DRAWINGS BY PETER BURCHARD

ADVENTURES

to Discovery

HERBERT AND MARJORIE KATZ

7045

COWARD-McCANN, INC., NEW YORK

Acknowledgments for photographs appear on page 242

Library of Congress Catalog Card Number: 70–84573

PRINTED IN THE UNITED STATES OF AMERICA
11up

For

Danny

and

Nina

ACKNOWLEDGMENTS

We thank all our museum friends. They have been marvelous. Enthusiastic, encouraging, and glad about what we were doing.

We thank Mary Gaver, former president of the American Library Association and professor at the Graduate School of Library Science at Rutgers State University, who advised us of the need for this book and encouraged us to write it.

We thank our editor, Alice Torrey, a knowledgeable taskmaster who knows what she wants and knows how to get it while remaining a friend.

CONTENTS

A WORD BEFORE YOU BEGIN

We hope this book will help you make four kinds of discoveries:

Discoveries about art, science, nature and history that may lead you into a lifelong interest in one or all of these fields.

Discoveries about the people who built some of our museum collections. Who they were. Why they started collecting.

Discoveries about how great art, science and history collections were accumulated and placed all over America. How America managed to grow so wonderfully museum-rich.

Discoveries about the basic ingredients of a museum adventure. How to concentrate on just one subject at a time. How to find what you are already interested in, and how to find something new. How to use the appendix of this book to locate a museum near you similar to one that is far away.

As you read this book, you may be surprised to find that a famous or favorite museum has been left out of the text (although you will probably find it in the listing at the back). The museums we have chosen are the ones that provided us with the best opportunities for describing the exciting variety of adventures we wanted to bring you.

We wish you the happiest of museum adventures.

HERBERT AND MARJORIE KATZ

Part I
HISTORY

1

THE CHARLESTON MUSEUM
Rutledge Avenue and Calhoun Street
Charleston, South Carolina 29401

THE PEALE MUSEUM
225 North Holliday Street
Baltimore, Maryland 21202

America's first museum—the Charleston Museum—began without any treasures to hang on its walls or put in its cupboards. It began with a picture of the head of a bird.

The picture was not an important work of art. It was really a scientific exhibit. One looked at it not to appreciate the technique of the artist, but to identify the species of the bird. The contributor was one of the local citizens who enjoyed collecting things related to nature or to his country's brief history.

The Charleston Museum, which opened three years before the Revolutionary War, was a democratic institution. It welcomed everyone. In all Europe there was no museum like it, no place where the public could enter without first obtaining special permission. Europe, of course, was rich in great collections of art. But they belonged to kings and princes and were intended only for their owners' pleasure. America, at that time, had none of these treas-

13

ures. But America was a land of excitement and discovery. There was great enthusiasm for collecting mineral specimens, maps, books, weapons, animal bones, furniture—anything at all that could be considered of "scientific" interest. In fact, the very habit of collecting was thought of as a scientific occupation.

At about the same time there lived in Philadelphia a portrait artist named Charles Willson Peale. During the Revolutionary War he served at Trenton, and became friendly with such military and political leaders as George Washington, Alexander Hamilton, Thomas Jefferson and others. He painted them all, and after the war hung their portraits in a gallery in his Philadelphia home. He was a scientist as well, and a tireless collector of rocks and minerals and stuffed and mounted animals.

This was before the time of public education and public libraries, and Peale decided to admit his fellow Philadelphians, for a fee, to his science collection and portrait gallery. He turned a wing of his house into a museum where visitors could see a picture called "The Staircase," so realistic that dogs would sometimes run against it trying to climb the steps. Visitors could also stare at an anteater, an armadillo and a jackal that produced cries loud enough and sharp enough to alarm the whole neighborhood. To the relief of Mrs. Peale and the family, the museum was eventually moved. It was set up in Independence Hall in 1802, where it grew bigger and more important.

President Jefferson saw to it that Indian costumes and small mammals and birds brought back from the Lewis and Clark Expedition to the Pacific coast went to Peale. Sea captains and other Americans traveling abroad brought back other things that swelled the collection.

In 1814, two of Peale's sons, Rembrandt and Rubens, followed in his footsteps and established a museum in Baltimore. Rembrandt Peale set out to improve the taste of the public both in the fine arts and in science. He created a Gallery of Heroes in which he

14

hung about fifty portraits of famous Americans. And among his natural history exhibits he placed a "stupendous Skeleton of the Mammoth," one of two mastodons the family had dug up in New Jersey. These were the first skeletons of prehistoric mammals to be reassembled and exhibited anywhere.

Rubens Peale was an expert taxidermist. He stuffed and mounted dead animals for exhibition, making them as lifelike as possible. He was also in charge of a sizable menagerie of live animals that included wolves, a fox, elk, a baboon, an eagle, turtles and a pair of alligators. Once the two brothers printed an advertisement in which they boasted of a young "LIVING TIGER which may be seen with perfect security by the most timorous."

It was necessary to advertise in order to attract paying customers. Although the Peales were all dedicated to educating their fellow citizens, they hoped to make a living from their museum. Soon Rembrandt and Rubens discovered that they had to add all sorts of curiosities to their collection to catch the eye of the public. In another advertisement they spoke of the "Head of a NEW ZEALAND CHIEF, very richly tattooed," a knife with ninety-eight blades, a mummified cat and chopsticks from China.

In 1816 Rembrandt demonstrated a practical method of using coal gas for lighting. The gas was made in the museum by an apparatus he had installed. It became the first building in Baltimore to be regularly lighted by gas. As a result, Rembrandt and five local merchants formed the Gas Light Company of Baltimore, the first such company in the United States. But the business was not financially successful.

Neither was the museum. Nothing they did could make it profitable. Before long, it was forced to close. The building, however, was left standing. From time to time it was used for community activities. And in 1931 it was reopened as a museum.

The Charleston Museum is the oldest in the country. It was established before any other. But a fire destroyed the original build-

Detail from "Exhuming the First American Mastodon"

ing. The oldest, still-standing museum building in America is the Peale in Baltimore.

Both of these are now museums of local history. The Charleston Museum's exhibits reflect life in the city and state over the years. One can find Revolutionary and Civil War swords, costumes from the period between 1815 and 1850, an apothecary shop that stood on the corner of Broad and King streets in 1781, an exhibit of the ornamental ironwork that still decorates many Charleston buildings and a hall of birds from North and South Carolina. Another display explains the planting and harvesting of rice, and the way it is brought to market. Rice is a major industry of the Carolina low

16

country. As part of the job of recording city history, the museum maintains two historic houses. One of them belonged to Thomas Heyward, a signer of the Declaration of Independence.

The Peale Museum has on display a model of Rembrandt's gas-making equipment and the actual bones of the famous mastodon skeleton. There is also Charles Willson Peale's painting of his family and friends digging up the skeleton. The painting is called "Exhuming the First American Mastodon." But basically the museum is devoted to preserving objects and documents important in the life and history of Baltimore. Thousands of lithographs, photographs, engravings, drawings and paintings are filed and displayed. The museum also maintains the historic Carroll Mansion, where Charles Carroll of Carrollton, the longest-surviving signer of the Declaration of Independence, spent his last years.

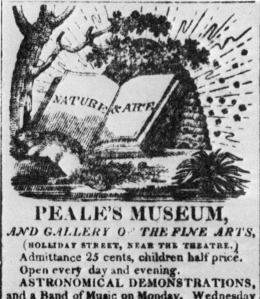

PEALE'S MUSEUM,
AND GALLERY OF THE FINE ARTS,
(HOLLIDAY STREET, NEAR THE THEATRE.)
Admittance 25 cents, children half price.
Open every day and evening.
ASTRONOMICAL DEMONSTRATIONS,
and a Band of Music on Monday, Wednesday
and Friday evenings—Tuesday, Thursday and
Saturday evenings, other PHILOSOPHICAL
EXPERIMENTS are exhibited.
PROFILES neatly executed and framed.
NB. A number of interesting LIVE ANI-
MALS have lately been added.   eo jy 23

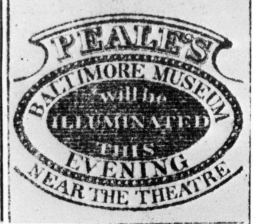

GAS LIGHTS.
NOTICE OF THE CLOSE OF THE SEASON.
The illumination of the Museum will be continued only for a few evenings longer for this season—but as a specimen of the manner in which the Front Room will be lighted, on the commencement of the next season, a CHANDELIER of fifty burners, executed by Mr BOUIS, is placed in the Quadruped Room, which for lightness and elegance is worthy of particular attention, and calculated to display the immense superiority of the Gas Light.

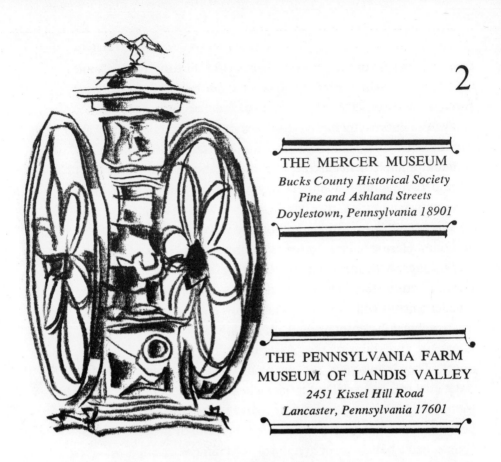

2

THE MERCER MUSEUM
Bucks County Historical Society
Pine and Ashland Streets
Doylestown, Pennsylvania 18901

THE PENNSYLVANIA FARM MUSEUM OF LANDIS VALLEY
2451 Kissel Hill Road
Lancaster, Pennsylvania 17601

In these two Pennsylvania museums you can see what life was really like for a pioneer family. Here you can discover that history is not just a matter of dates and battles. History is about people of years gone by, and about how they lived.

When America was still a wilderness, the basic problems of finding food, shelter and clothing had to be solved day after day after day. Imagine a world without electricity, automobiles, running water, supermarkets or telephones. You are standing in a huge forest without a house or a road in sight. You are the head of a family, with a wife and children to provide for. What will you do for a home, for protection from cold and rain? How will you get from one place to another? How will you provide the necessities of life for your family?

18

The Mercer Museum displays some 30,000 simple hand tools and implements used by Pennsylvanians before 1820. Many were brought by early settlers from their native European lands. Some show little improvement over those dug up by archeologists at the sites of prehistoric settlements in Europe. It is hard to believe, but some farm implements used at the time of the Revolutionary War were actually almost identical to those used thousands of years earlier.

The ground floor of the museum is devoted mostly to household activities. Here you can see utensils for making butter and cheese and for preserving meats and fruits before there were refrigerators, freezers and tin cans. Three period rooms—a kitchen, a parlor, and a bedchamber—will show you what it might have been like to live in an eighteenth-century house. A display of a glassblower's tools is part of an exhibit of the flasks, decanters and bottles he produced. These containers, tableware and decorative pieces meant a great deal to a housewife at a time when glass was more attractive than strictly functional tinware or coarse pottery, and cost less than pewter or china. There is even an exhibit of bathtubs. No one, of course, had a bathroom or hot and cold running water.

On the next three floors are implements used by farmers and craftsmen. The different jobs on a farm—threshing, winnowing, harvesting, beekeeping and animal husbandry, for example—each required special equipment. You will discover the tools and see the finished work of the wagon builder and wheelwright, the blacksmith, iron molder, potter, brickmaker, carpenter, the man who made combs from animal horns, the boot- and shoemaker and others whose skills and products made a hard life a little bit easier.

The lady of the house had to make all the clothing for her family: spinning wool and flax into thread, weaving thread into cloth, and then sewing the garments. Spinning, weaving and sewing equipment is displayed, along with some of the fabrics and clothes made by pioneer women.

19

In the large center courtyard are the things that are too big to be kept inside the museum's rooms. Here you will find some of the vehicles that carried people, farm produce and handcrafted articles from one place to another. Land vehicles were horse-drawn. Boats had to be paddled. You will see a stagecoach, Conestoga wagons, a whaleboat, some dugout canoes and fire engines. Several types of mill turned by waterpower to grind flour or saw lumber, and such oversize implements as winnowing machines, hay rakes and ox yokes are in the courtyard. Here too are a horse mounting block, tools for rope and harness making and some bicycles.

Most of these were collected by Dr. Henry Chapman Mercer, an archeologist who was a founder of the County Historical Society. He thought his collection would bring to life a time that we know only by reading about it, and he built the large, towered museum in which it is displayed.

Two brothers collected the quarter of a million objects that fill the Pennsylvania Farm Museum. While they were still in their teens, George and Henry Landis began accumulating used home and farm implements. That was in the 1880's. They eventually crammed their family farmhouse and barns with pianos and candle molds, pots and patchwork quilts, tin trays and wooden Indians, rifles and rakes, buggies and sleighs. By the time they died in the 1950's, they were known to their neighbors as the Penny Men, because they would go to every local sale and auction, offering one cent for whatever was still unsold at the end. In this way they gathered quantities of everyday articles, including 1,000 pairs of wrought-iron hinges and a dozen spinning wheels, as well as such truly extraordinary things as a washing machine that was worked by dog power.

For several generations, the Landis family had been farming just north of Lancaster, Pennsylvania. In 1815, Jacob Landis, a great-granduncle of the brothers, had built a brick two-story farmhouse. Now, as part of the museum, it is the center of a small farm that is

20

actually worked as it might have been in the early nineteenth century. Among the antiques in the farmhouse are a grandfather clock, a pianoforte and a fireplace framed with purple tiles. Nearby is the small "Grossmutter" or Grandmother's house, where older members of the Landis family lived. A barn and two log houses are also on the museum grounds.

A short distance away is the 1870 home where the two brothers spent most of their lives. In it are the furnishings that belonged to the family in those years—such things as brass oil lamps, an old-fashioned phonograph, and painted furniture. In the large Yellow Barn, shops of several nineteenth-century craftsmen have been rebuilt. Set up and ready for use are all the tools needed by a butcher, a coppersmith, a blacksmith, a tinsmith and a leatherworker. On certain weekends in June and October, you can see the equipment

actually used by a potter shaping mugs and pitchers and a carpenter working wood with old hand tools.

Steps in the making of textiles are demonstrated in the Red Barn. Flax and wool are spun into yarn, the yarn is woven into cloth, and the cloth is dyed and then sewn. Cloth woven here has been used to curtain many windows of the museum buildings, and for the cover on the old Conestoga wagon in the wagon shed. Conestoga wagons originated in the early eighteenth century in southeastern Pennsylvania. They are named for a group of Indians who once lived in the region. At first they were used to transport farm produce and equipment locally. As the frontier was pushed farther and farther west, the wagons carried heavy manufactured goods across the Alleghenies. The characteristic curve of the wagon base, designed so that it was higher at the front and back than in the middle, prevented bulky goods from falling against the wooden tail gate and breaking it on up- or downhill roads. The fabric covering of the wagon was shaped to follow that curve.

22

At the museum, a shed holds sleighs used for winter travel, a plow designed by Thomas Jefferson and other farm equipment. In the warmer months, reapers, rakes and harrows are among the farm equipment displayed outdoors. Nearby are a country store with the post office which was a part of it, and a tavern with a huge fireplace in its kitchen. Summer visitors may find a baker making crisp apple dumplings in an oven outside the tavern. A gunshop holds hunting, fishing and trapping gear and a collection of Pennsylvania rifles known for their accuracy and brass ornaments.

Although most of the Farm Museum exhibits illustrate the rural life that was familiar to many Americans during the nineteenth century, there are also reminders of the very special population of this part of Pennsylvania. The area was settled by German immigrants, who came to be known as Pennsylvania Dutch. The second floor of the tavern is devoted to the colorful folk art of these people. China, painted tin trays, wooden chests and boxes are decorated with designs of birds, hearts, flowers and vines. The two designs painted over the door of the large barn are hex signs. The Pennsylvania Dutch believed these signs could ward off evil and bring good fortune.

3

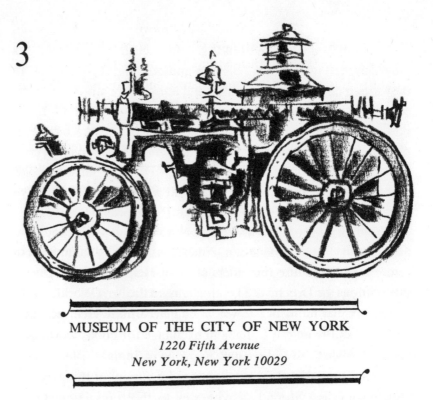

MUSEUM OF THE CITY OF NEW YORK
1220 Fifth Avenue
New York, New York 10029

There are two ways of visiting the Museum of the City of New York. One is to come here for a better understanding of how New York grew from a Dutch colony to a powerful metropolis. The other is to enjoy the place as a kind of overgrown treasure house of dolls, fire engines, little window displays, make-believe stores and make-believe rooms.

In a basement gallery you can stare up at a brass-trimmed, huge-wheeled old fire engine from the 1880's. Upstairs you can peer into a small showcase in which a doll-size figure of Marconi is shown making the first "absolute demonstration to the Western world of the value of the wireless" telegraph. On the same floor you can examine an exhibit of priceless silver and jewelry that belonged to the old New York families, the Van Cortlandts and Schuylers.

But the museum's most dramatic exhibit is its new Dutch Gallery, which tells the story of New Amsterdam.

24

The entrance to the Dutch Gallery is dark, but you can soon see glowing colors showing through the blackness. The story of New York's beginnings as New Amsterdam is about to unfold. Fluorescent paints have been used for diagrams, pictures, maps and a printed text that tell how the Netherlands came to be a world power. Ultraviolet light brings out the electric yellows, reds, greens and blues that tell about scientific advances—especially in astronomy and navigation—that made an age of exploration possible, and tell of how a seafaring, shipbuilding people developed trade.

In a lighted case you see the gear of a sixteenth-century soldier; nearby a display of navigational instruments, and then models of three ships, including the *Half Moon* of Henry Hudson. On his explorations the Dutch based their claims in the New World.

The familiar moment in 1626 when Peter Minuit received Manhattan Island from the Indians in exchange for goods worth $24 has been realistically re-created. A group of Indians listens as the governor offers them blankets, pots and a variety of things, while Dutchmen stand around as witnesses to the transaction. Other scenes are re-created—an Indian village, and Stone Street, the first paved street in New Amsterdam.

In the center of the gallery is a bastion of Fort Amsterdam, complete with a cannon. The stone walls of the fort are partly surrounded by the pointed wood poles of a stockade. You can climb up the stairs into the fort, and look out over its stone walls to a view of the city that surrounds you on all sides. This painted cityscape, called a cyclorama because it circles the fort, is based on a town plan drawn more than 300 years ago. It shows every building and street. Indians, housewives and solid burghers mingle on the footpaths.

Dutch political control ended in 1664 when the English captured the colony. But the Dutch remained and continued to influence daily life.

At the opposite end of the first floor is a hall devoted to high-lights of the city's life from 1800 to the present. In the center of this gallery is a streetcar in use 100 years ago. It was drawn by horses along a route that led from Broadway at City Hall up Eighth Avenue to Columbus Circle. Near it is an ambulance, also horse-drawn, that served Bellevue Hospital in 1898.

A small display shows Central Park on a snowy day in 1865. Skaters are out, and so are carriages, their wheels removed and run-ners attached to convert them into sleighs. Another scene repro-duces the first Woolworth's, which came to the city in 1897. Finely dressed ladies stand at counters laden with lengths of fabric, teakettles and other merchandise. A red and gold sign hanging above their heads announces: NOTHING IN THIS STORE OVER 10 CENTS.

26

Central Park, 1865 (diorama)

Not far away are two exhibits of New York's most famous landmarks, the Statue of Liberty and the Empire State Building.

Bartholdi, the sculptor who created the Statue of Liberty, made an early study of it that is here. In this model, Liberty holds a broken chain in her left hand, symbolizing the broken bonds of oppression. The idea was dropped and Liberty now holds a symbolic volume, the *Book of the Rights of Man*. The Empire State Building is shown during construction in 1930. Most of the figures on the eighty-third floor riveting together the steel framework of the world's tallest building are actual portraits of the real workmen.

An elevator ride up to the third floor of the museum will put you on a street of a century ago, lined with shops and lit by a gas lamp. Rows of ladies' and children's shoes fill the window of the Boots and Shoe Emporium. All sorts of bonnets, a black lace parasol, fans and a small beaded handbag are in the milliner's shop. In a toy store are dishes, dolls, a tin wagon, books, cards and games. One shopwindow is full of dolls' heads, made of china with the features and hair painted on. If you were a little girl about 100

years ago, and someone wanted to give you a very special present, you might have been taken to this store and allowed to select your favorite doll's head. The rest of the doll would have been made to your order. The arms, legs and body, made of cloth and stuffed with sawdust, would be fastened to the head through holes below the shoulders. Then the doll would be dressed in the clothes you had chosen.

Also on the third floor is a room lined with cabinets and shelves. This too might have been a toyshop years ago. It is crowded with dolls. You will find too a toy fire engine, a police patrol wagon and an ice wagon, all made of iron. A group of circus toys includes a bandwagon, acrobats on a revolving wheel, an animal cage and acrobats dancing on a cart. A complete circus, with big top, performers and animals, that would delight any child of any century is set up nearby. Other nineteenth-century toys include a box of magic tricks, marbles, puzzles, farm animals carved of wood, paper dolls (some of them lovingly hand-painted by the little girls to whom they belonged) and a board game in which players try to reach the Mansion of Happiness, after traveling through indescribable hazards.

In another gallery, visitors are reminded that New York's importance as the center of the nation's business life depends on communications. The first regular postal service in the colony dates back to 1673, when the first mail courier mounted his horse in lower New York and set off on a trip to Boston that would take about a week. A model of this significant event shows the governor bidding farewell to that pioneer mailman with prominent citizens standing by, wishing him a successful journey.

Modern business depends even more on the telephone. In the museum is a model of the telephone through which Alexander Graham Bell first transmitted speech in 1875, with a portrait of the inventor. Bell demonstrated his invention to New Yorkers for the first time in 1877. Here you can see a group of distinguished scien-

28

tists, gathered in a room of a hotel at Broadway and Eleventh Street, hearing a cornet solo being played across the river in Brooklyn.

This must have been a convincing demonstration, for within five years a central telephone exchange was serving the city. On display is a large wall telephone from this period. It is made of wood, and was powered by its own electric generator, which had to be cranked by the caller before he could reach the operator at Central who placed his call.

On March 11, 1888, 22 inches of snow fell on the city in twenty-four hours. This was the famous Blizzard of Eighty-eight, and a model of a city street shows the snow piled up nearly to the ground-floor windows of the buildings. By that time the city was dependent on the telegraph and the telephone, and a mass of wires hung overhead. Weighted down with snow and pushed by high winds, the wires snapped and broke during the storm, and communications completely broke down.

The museum's collection contains more than 1,400 dresses and untold numbers of men's and children's garments, but only a few are on display. Most are in garment bags stored away upstairs on the fourth floor. All these garments belonged to New Yorkers, and some were worn on historic occasions. One outfit, a man's purple velvet knee breeches and matching coat and vest, was worn to George Washington's inaugural ball. And a silver gown was worn to a ball given in honor of the Marquis de Lafayette. A collection like this never stops growing. Recently, apparel from the "swinging sixties" has been added, including a paper dress and a Beatles wig.

It really doesn't matter where you start in this museum. You're sure to find more than one favorite spot.

29

4

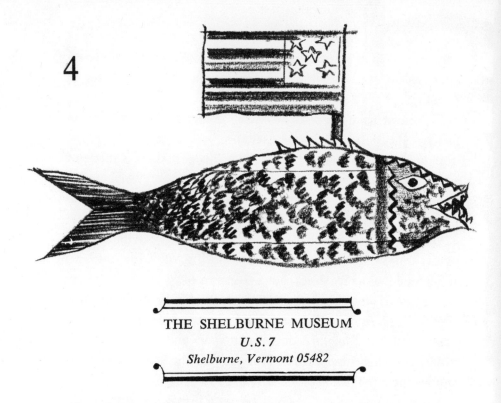

THE SHELBURNE MUSEUM
U.S. 7
Shelburne, Vermont 05482

Sometime around 1890 a little girl growing up in New York received her first doll. As she grew older, she was given more dolls, and her grandmother made clothes for them.

Every little girl would like to have lots of dolls, but few can have as many as they want. Electra Havemayer's father was a very rich man, and by the time she was a young lady, she had hundreds and hundreds of dolls. She had dolls made of wood and wax, of papier-mâché and china, of rags, rubber, rawhide, seashells and all sorts of other materials. Some were dressed in ball gowns of satin, trimmed with lace and pearls. Some were so small they could rest on her fingers, and some were as tall as she was. Not all had been made for children; some were miniature fashion models displaying dress styles from which women could order. Some were music boxes, and some were animated to perform a dance or trick when a key was turned. Some were new, and some were very, very old.

30

After Electra Havemayer married J. Watson Webb, she was taken to visit her husband's family in the town of Shelburne, Vermont. There she saw an old brick house that no one had lived in for years. This would be her summer house, the young couple's second home.

For her first home, Electra had chosen furniture made by American craftsmen years before. She had bought patchwork quilts of fabric scraps stitched into marvelously colorful and intricate patterns, painted store signs and carved eagles, hand-painted wallpaper and hooked rugs—all made in an earlier America. Such things are called Americana. Electra and her husband furnished their summer home with these things, too.

The urge that had started the girl collecting hundreds and hundreds of dolls led her as a grown woman to buy thousands and thousands of old, wonderful things made by hand. Things made of glass, pottery, pewter and wood, as well as tools, pictures, fabrics and furniture, filled her attic storage room and spilled over into the wings that from time to time were added to the little house. Electra Webb bought Americana as though she were stocking a department store. Then she decided that she would have a museum.

New England's yesterdays come alive beyond Route 7 and over the covered bridge that leads to the Shelburne Museum. Covered bridges were once common in this region. In the years before modern steel construction, a roof protected the hand-hewn wooden timbers of the roadway from being destroyed by the heat of the sun and the dampness of rain and snow. In a time of horse-drawn vehicles, the protected sides of the bridge kept horses from bolting in panic at the sight of the rivers or lakes they had to cross.

The bridge now at Shelburne was built in 1845 over a river near the town of Cambridge, 36 miles away. But after more than 100 years a modern four-lane bridge was needed for heavy highway traffic. The old wooden one, which had only two lanes and a footpath, was to be demolished.

32

This might have become one of the thousands of covered bridges that have been lost forever if Mr. and Mrs. Webb hadn't acted fast. They moved the bridge to their museum grounds, where it was rebuilt timber by timber. A lily pond was specially dug for the 168-foot bridge to cross. Today it is one of more than thirty structures that have been moved here from other parts of the state.

The first building moved to Shelburne was a little one-room brick schoolhouse. The Webbs discovered it in the town of Vergennes, where it had been built in 1830. Mrs. Webb found desks and blackboards from the same period. She even searched out children's jackets to hang on pegs, and actual copy-books (as notebooks were called then) and drawings made by children 100 years ago. A pupil who forgot to do his homework, or who disturbed the other students, would have been made to sit on a high stool in a corner of the schoolroom, wearing a dunce cap; you can see the

stool and the cone-shaped cap made from a newspaper of 1868.
You can also see the old stove that provided heat on cold winter
days. Imagine how the children clustered around it in the early-
morning chill, or ran to it when they came in from play in the snow-
covered yard.

The Stagecoach Inn is another building that was moved from its
original location. It was built during the Revolution, on a road that
became the main stage route between Montreal and southern New
England, and over the years it sheltered many travelers. When it
was brought to Shelburne, it had to be completely dismantled.
Forty thousand bricks and ten fireplaces were among the parts that
were moved and put together again. When wooden window cas-
ings or chair rails had to be repaired, the old carpenters' tools in
Mrs. Webb's collection were used to do the job.

Today the Stagecoach Inn holds one of the nation's finest collections of folk art. The wooden figures—a horse or a graceful lady
—were shaped by self-taught artisans whose only training was
years and years of practice. All these pieces were originally designed to serve a practical purpose. The ladies were ships' figureheads, bringing good luck to their owners. The cigar-store Indians

34

advertised tobacco; the small tin horses perched handsomely on weather vanes and the larger wooden ones are from a carousel. Toy animals and wagons were whittled by a village carpenter in his spare time; other toys were cut from scrap metal by the village tinsmith.

Everywhere there are eagles—of wood, cast iron, papier-mâché and tin. This symbol of the young nation was a popular decoration for public buildings, and the early craftsmen created them in every size and pose. Largest is the one which once guarded the shipyards at Portsmouth, New Hampshire. It measures 16 feet from the tip of one outstretched wing to the tip of the other, and it towers over the ballroom of the Stagecoach Inn where it is displayed.

In another house of about the same age there is a display of cooking, cleaning and sewing utensils that tells a story of hard work and ingenuity.

Nearby is a general store that was the only shop for a whole village. It is so well supplied that when you go in, you are tempted to buy crackers from the barrel standing on the floor, or choose something from the candy counter. In an alcove is a barbershop; shelves on the wall hold dozens of shaving mugs. Each patron kept one there for his own use. An almanac for the year 1842 lies on the table where waiting customers would look for something to read. And a high chair that swivels stands ready for a child coming for his first haircut. In another alcove of the store is the village post office; upstairs are the offices of a doctor and a dentist.

As the Webbs added buildings and furnishings to their museum, they became increasingly interested in all sorts of early American structures. And just as the covered bridge found its way here, so did an old lighthouse that had been maintained by the Coast Guard in the middle of nearby Lake Champlain. From Lake Champlain came also the S.S. *Ticonderoga,* a side-wheeler steamboat that had carried passengers and freight for many years. The job of moving it over dry land to the museum took sixty-six days. Now you can

35

board it and visit the room that Mrs. Webb furnished as a honeymoon suite. A big brass bed, an old bureau, a chair with a richly embroidered seat, a bridal bouquet and even nightclothes for the bride and groom are all in place, just as though they were waiting to be used.

There is much, much more here, and it would take several days of visiting to see properly the old slate jailhouse, the home furnished as though a retired sea captain were living in it, the blacksmith's shop, the meetinghouse, several barns, a sawmill and a hunting lodge. A collection of carriages, sleighs and wagons, all used in the years before the automobile, are in one large barn. Many of them belonged to Mr. Webb's family. A railroad station and steam locomotive, fire-fighting equipment and a snowplow are also here as part of the story of early transportation.

In the old brick house known as the Variety Unit are several of Mrs. Webb's favorite collections. She was particularly fond of pewter, a practical metal alloy made of tin, copper and other metals. It was called "poor man's silver." Handsome pewter vases, pitchers, mugs and bowls are displayed in old pine cupboards, as they might have been in a country dining room; a table in the same

1846 water pumper

room is set with pewter knives and forks and spoons, plates, pitchers and serving dishes. In other rooms are collections of glass and pottery, including a fine group of Toby jugs—those large mugs in the shape of jolly men. A collection of old toys includes miniature stagecoaches, trolleys and fire engines, as well as penny banks, a toy Civil War cannon, a mechanical cobbler who nods as he hammers on a piece of shoe leather and an elaborate model train. And then of course there are those dolls that started Electra Havemayer Webb on her career of collecting Americana and building a museum.

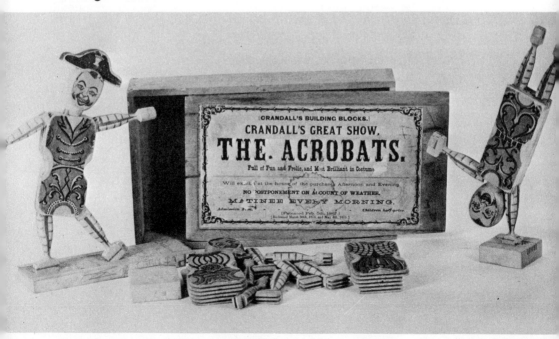

5

NEBRASKA STATE HISTORICAL SOCIETY MUSEUM
1500 R Street
Lincoln, Nebraska 68508

Nebraska's museum set itself the task of telling the state's story "from the Atlatl to the Atlas." The atlatl was a throwing-stick used by prehistoric Indians. It gave extra thrust for hurling a sharpened stone missile. The Atlas, of course, is the space-age missile that is kept ready on Air Force bases in Nebraska today. The span in time from atlatl to Atlas is about 10,000 years.

The first and longest part of the story being told here is unfolded in the Indian Gallery in the west wing of the first floor. Here we go back to prehistory, a distant past that we know about only from the things people left behind them. (The more recent past, made up of events written about by people alive when the events took place, is history.)

Scientific detectives who discover clues to prehistory from things made and used in those distant times are called archeologists. In

Nebraska, archeologists, digging deep in the earth, have come upon pieces of broken pottery, fishhooks, scrapers, pipes, ornaments and all sorts of other things made by ancient Indians. Such man-made things are called artifacts. From them it is possible to piece together the story of what life was like on the Great Plains 9,000 years before the white man began exploring the region.

The earliest Indians here were nomads who lived by hunting. These wanderers moved from place to place in pursuit of game. They lived simply, chipping stone to fashion spearpoints which they attached with strips of animal skin and sinew to the wooden atlatls.

About 6,000 years later other Indians arrived in the region. They built houses of grassy earth over a framework of poles. They made large clay pots, with pointed bottoms and a rough-textured surface. A display labeled "From Archeological Excavation into the History of a People" shows some of the things archeologists have found, and what they tell about the pottery makers. Small lengths and disks of carved bone have been strung on leather strips or thongs to form necklaces and hair ornaments. Bits of broken pottery have been matched up and glued together to form the whole cooking vessel. Fish and animal bones, seeds and corncobs tell about the food of those long-ago people. A heap of stones covered with charcoal is evidence of a campfire. Pieces of stone and bone, carved to a point or chipped and scraped to a sharp edge, give us an idea of what the tools and weapons of these early Indians may have been like.

By the time the white man arrived, the Pawnee, Omaha, Ponca, Oto and Missouri tribes were living in villages in what are now the eastern and central parts of the state. They lived in circular earth lodges, and tended large gardens of squash, beans, pumpkins and corn. This diet was supplemented by the meat from two buffalo hunts a year. The buffalo also provided hides for robes, boxes, medicine bundles, saddle pads and other articles. Most of these

39

were decorated with painted designs, porcupine quills and beads. The "scalp shirt" worn by Ponca Chief Standing Bear is one of the more elaborate examples of hidework on display. Among its ornaments are dozens of hair tufts the chief cut from the heads of captured enemies.

The warlike Sioux, Arapaho and Cheyenne lived in western Nebraska. They were primarily hunters, following buffalo herds on their swift horses. Their homes were tepees, easily taken down when it came time to move to a new hunting ground. A display case labeled "Dressing to Kill" shows some of the finery of the Sioux brave—a large feathered headdress, a shield of painted buffalo hide, a tomahawk. In the next display the story of Sioux clothing is continued with fashions worn by squaws to catch a warrior's eye. A beaded and fringed dress made of buffalo hide bleached almost white, a brightly decorated case for carrying a papoose and painted skin leggings are among the Indian lady's finery.

Before going across the first floor to the Pioneer Gallery, which tells of the changes brought by the arrival of the white man, you might go upstairs to the west wing of the second floor. Here are several rooms from the past, with furnishings that once belonged to Nebraska pioneer families.

The soddy was once the most usual type of dwelling on the flat prairie landscape. Farmers attracted by the government's offer of free land to anyone who would live on it and cultivate it settled Nebraska. Those who came here from the East to stake their claims under the Homestead Act of 1862 found the soil hard and the climate harsh. The only building material at hand on the dry, windy and practically treeless plains was the earth. And so the settlers did just as the Indians before them had done: They built houses from the hard soil. They cut large, rectangular clumps of sod right out of the earth and stacked them, with the grass side down, to form one-room homes. More sod blocks laid over cedar poles formed the roofs.

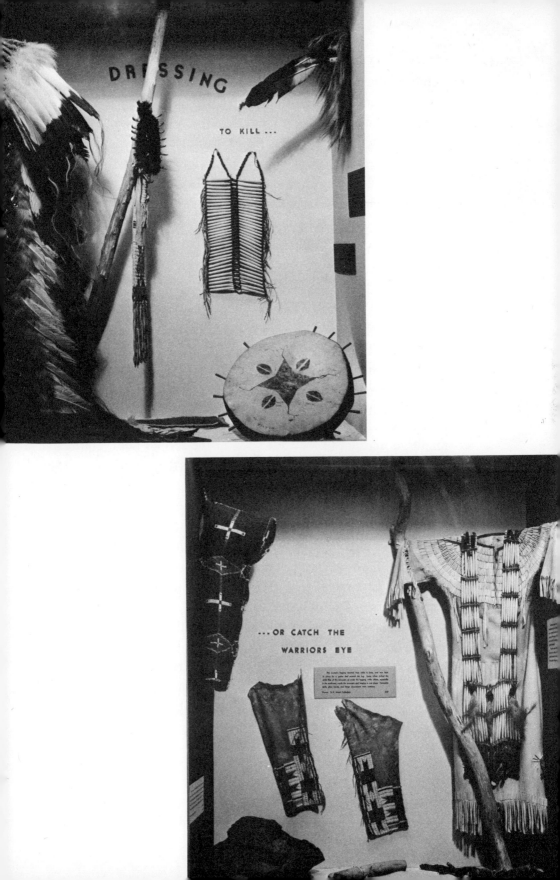

DRESSING

TO KILL ...

...OR CATCH THE
WARRIORS EYE

The soddy's thick walls gave good protection from the weather, keeping the house warm in winter and cool in summer. Inside, the walls were daubed with clay, and usually whitewashed. But the roof leaked terribly. And dirt, blown in through the windows, filtering down from the roof and kicked up from the earth floor, was a constant problem. A handmade rag carpet on the floor helped keep dust from rising. More prosperous settlers built a ceiling of wooden planks under the roof, and laid planks for a floor, too.

The women made bright curtains for the windows and gay quilts to cover the beds. Almost everything the pioneer family used was handmade, from the clothes they wore to the rough cake of yellow soap on the washstand. A few treasured belongings—a small cabinet or perhaps a clock or a framed family portrait—might have been brought from the East. But the basic pieces of furniture—bedstead, chairs, table—were made by the man of the house.

The most important thing the settler had to buy was the hay-burning stove. In a land without trees, dry grass was the most usual fuel. Weeds and straw were also burned. The old hay burner in the museum's soddy provided heat for the house as well as for cooking.

In the Pioneer Gallery on the first floor you can see what a sod house looked like from the outside. A pioneer housewife is at work laundering and cooking while her children do necessary chores.

Even before the pioneer settlers, fur traders were busy in Nebraska. They came up the Missouri River, along the eastern boundary of the state, in the spring. Their long keelboats carried blankets and beads, guns and metal pots for trading with Indian fur trappers. In the fall the traders would go back down the river, the keelboats laden with furs. A view of the interior of a trading post shows the trader making a record of the transaction in his ledger as an Indian selects his purchases. Beaver skins that the Indian has brought in are on the counter. Shelves in the little log-walled room display plates and pitchers, bottles and pots.

Another display, "The Buffalo Hunters," tells a sad story. A hunter crouches, rifle in hand and gun in holster, searching out his prey on a plain covered with animal bones. The vast herds of these great animals would be cut down in a few years by greedy gunmen eager to sell buffalo skins. Other exhibits in the Pioneer Gallery tell of the U.S. Army's cavalry and its role in the Indian wars, of the Pony Express and of such Old West heroes as "Wild Bill" Hickok.

The Historical Society's library, on the second floor of the museum, is a treasure-trove of books and newspapers, letters, magazines, papers and photographs. Among them is the diary of John Bourke, a cavalryman who talked with the Indians and wrote about his conversations with them.

A Cheyenne called Five Crow told Bourke a story of how horses came to the warrior tribes: One day a Cheyenne maiden wandered away from her home. Her trail was followed for a great distance by her relatives. When they saw that her footprints disappeared at the edge of a large lake, they began to mourn. Then she returned, leading a fine black stallion, the first the Indians had ever seen. She told them she was now married to a white man, and he had given her the horse. Soon after that, she came again with a mare. From this mare and the stallion came all the horses of the Cheyenne, Sioux and Arapaho.

The Indian legend is probably a poetic version of the truth. The white man of the story was most likely a Spaniard. Most historians agree that the Plains Indians, who became famous as horsemen, got their first horses from the Spanish settlements in the Southwest sometime in the eighteenth century.

43

6

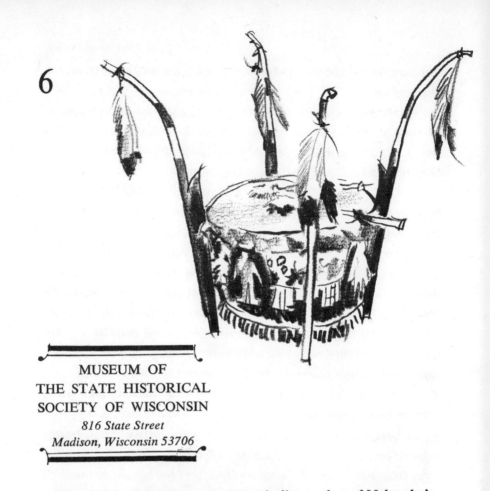

MUSEUM OF
THE STATE HISTORICAL
SOCIETY OF WISCONSIN
816 State Street
Madison, Wisconsin 53706

Wisconsin's past is in many ways similar to that of Nebraska's. The first Indians to come to the state were nomadic hunters. Later arrivals were pottery makers and farmers. European explorers found Indians who farmed, hunted and fished and lived in villages. Wisconsin's first white settlers were fur traders. They were followed by pioneers who preferred farming. And so, in some ways, Wisconsin's history resembles Nebraska's. But many details are different.

Digging in very early prehistoric Indian graves near Lake Superior, archeologists discovered copper tools and ornaments buried along with human skeletons. These tools belonged to the so-called Old Copper People, who hammered copper nuggets into

44

spearpoints and beads. They were among the world's first metal-workers.

A somewhat later prehistoric group in Wisconsin were the Mound Builders. They left behind large, low earth mounds in the shape of animals. When archeologists dug into them, they found that the mounds, like gravestones, marked burial places. The Mound Builders were farmers, and were particularly skilled in making small stone carvings of animal and human figures.

About 1,000 years ago, there came a group of Indians who lived in houses made of young trees plastered with mud and roofed over with bark. They built large temples shaped like Egyptian pyramids, but cut off at the top to form flat roofs. Because these temples seemed similar to those of the Mexican Aztecs, the fortified city built by the Wisconsin group was called Aztalan by the nineteenth-century scientists who came to study it. Now scientists know that there was no relationship between the two.

The Indian tribes who lived in Wisconsin when the first white men arrived included the Winnebago, Menominee, Chippewa,

Head of Woodland Indian woman

Potowatomi, Sauk and Fox. These were the people whose winter home was the wigwam, a rounded hut with a bark roof. In the museum's real wigwam you can see how poles set in the ground were bent and tied together at the top. This curved framework gave the wigwam its conical shape.

In the museum you will find exhibits showing all these stages of Indian life in Wisconsin, along with many artifacts that tell what Indian life was like. Here are tools and ornaments of the Old Copper People, polished stone and bone articles made by Mound Builders and the pottery and clothing of more recent tribes.

Unlike Nebraska, Wisconsin is a land of trees and rivers. The museum's full-size log cabin is a typical pioneer home in a forest area. You can see building tools the settlers used, and how they placed the logs.

Many of the pioneers, learning of large lead deposits, stayed to become miners. They were called badgers because often they lived in the mine shafts just as a badger lives in the tunnels he digs. From this came Wisconsin's nickname, the Badger State. Exhibits show the mining activities of frontier life, too.

Not all settlers came as farmers or miners. Many were attracted to the growing towns. They were shopkeepers, blacksmiths or carpenters, or they may have been teachers, preachers or lawyers. When Wisconsin became a state in 1848, a new wave of settlers headed for Madison, the capital, seeking government employment. Among them was a man named Lyman Copeland Draper, who hoped to be appointed state librarian.

As a boy in western New York, Draper had listened to tales told by his father and grandfather about the Revolutionary War and the War of 1812. He was fascinated by them. When he grew older, he realized that these true stories would be lost forever if someone did not write them down. He set himself that task, and the added task of gathering as many stories from other people as he could.

He traveled the Appalachian frontier, becoming friendly with

Preparing a diorama

strangers, asking them questions and keeping a record of what they told him. Sometimes he was fortunate enough to come upon an old soldier who had kept a diary of his wartime adventures, or a housewife who had saved letters from her husband and sons. Promising to publish these records in a book he was planning to write, Draper usually succeeded in getting them as a gift. By the time he came to Madison, he had filled more than 10,000 notebook pages and had nearly as many pages of diaries and letters.

Draper did not get the job of state librarian, but he did join the new State Historical Society. Almost immediately he became its librarian and chief officer. He began to build the society's collection of documents and books, as he had his own. During the Civil War he collected everything in sight—flags, money and uniforms of both sides, and even cannonballs. Of course he gathered diaries and letters as well.

For more than thirty years he worked to develop the Historical Society. He never did write the book he had planned, but his own

47

invaluable library of books and papers, which he gave the society, made up for that.

Part of the story of Wisconsin's heritage is told at branch museums maintained by the Historical Society. The Circus World Museum is in Baraboo, a town 40 miles north of Madison that was for many years the winter quarters of the early Ringling Brothers' Circus. Every year, from May through September, you can see the large collection of circus wagons, a menagerie, real circus acts, sideshows, a big top and a circus train; there are even traditional circus treats—peanuts, cotton candy and pink lemonade!

At the western side of the state, near where the Wisconsin River meets the Mississippi, is the city of Prairie du Chien. Here, after the War of 1812, American troops built Fort Crawford. Some years later a new fortification was built elsewhere, and the first Fort Crawford was put up for sale.

The buyer was a young fur trader, Hercules Dousman. Alongside the fort's blockhouse he built his elegant home, naming it Villa Louis. It became the center of social and business affairs as the city of Prairie du Chien grew up around it.

Villa Louis is now maintained by the State Historical Society and is open to the public. You can see the glittering crystal chandeliers, paintings and porcelains, silk and velvet upholstery and other fine furnishings that later members of the Dousman family have treasured. The carriage house has been turned into a museum telling of the city's past as an Indian village, fur-trading center and military post. It tells also of the time when the railroad arrived, connecting the community with the rest of the state and nation. And the old fort has been excavated and partially reconstructed.

The story of a pioneer family is told at the Old Wade House in Greenbush, in the eastern part of the state. Sylvanus Wade, his wife and their nine children came to Wisconsin in 1844, built a log cabin and settled down. A year later a road was cut through the wilderness, following a trail that went right past Wade's doorstep.

Wade opened a blacksmith shop to provide services he knew
would be needed by stagecoaches and freight wagons and the
horses that pulled them. His son-in-law, Charles Robinson, built a
sawmill on a nearby river. From it came the fine butternut wood
planks he used for his home. Wade and Robinson also put up an
inn called Wade House where drivers, their passengers, and horses
could rest overnight.

Today at Greenbush you can visit the Butternut House and the
Wade House. When it was decided to use these buildings as museums, their foundations were crumbling, the supporting beams
were sagging, and layers of paint covered the hand-carved pine and
butternut woodwork. The old furniture, dusty and damaged, was
heaped in the ballroom of the inn. Only months of careful work
brought everything back to its original condition. Now you can see

49

the dining room, ready to receive hungry travelers; the taproom where a man could get a drink, chat, and have a game of checkers; the bedrooms, parlor, kitchens, and the ballroom itself.

Nelson Dewey, Wisconsin's first governor, built another fine house on his plantation at Cassville. It overlooks the Mississippi in the southwestern corner of the state. His enormous barn has become the State Farm Museum, where a great collection of tools makes clear changes in ways of farming. The governor's home can be visited also. Afterward you can climb into a horse-drawn bus and ride across a covered bridge to Stonefield Village.

Here is a rural community of the 1890's, complete with stores, school, church, barbershop and so on. Although this is a village built to be a museum, a village that never really was, it is like one that might have been. You are asked to imagine that the first settlers in Stonefield came in the 1830's. The blacksmith's shop, general store, bank and church are built in the style of those early frontier days. If this had been a real place, the buildings would still have been standing, still in use, in the 1890's—the period shown at the village today.

The unique fact about Stonefield Village is that it changes regularly. It always shows life about seventy-five years in the past. Now at Stonefield, the first telephone exchange has recently been installed. The first automobile, a Model T, will arrive in about fifteen years. You can still see the old pharmacy, not yet replaced by a drugstore. Rows of chemists' jars stand on shelves behind the counter where the pharmacist mixes medicines, using a large mortar and pestle. On the wall are advertisements for patent medicines—in one of them a grumpy-looking baby asks for "Dr. Stork's Baby Cough Syrup."

About seventy-five years from now, Stonefield Village will have today's television sets, supermarkets and automobiles—all of which will seem terribly old-fashioned to anyone who visits the town.

50

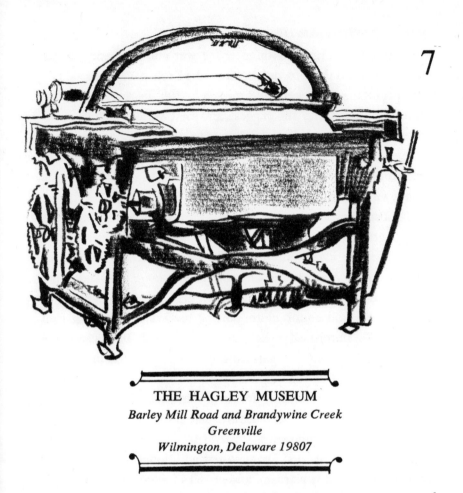

THE HAGLEY MUSEUM
Barley Mill Road and Brandywine Creek
Greenville
Wilmington, Delaware 19807

On the first day of the nineteenth century, a man named Eleuthère Irénée Du Pont and his family arrived in the United States. They had come from France where Du Pont worked under the great chemist Lavoisier. Lavoisier was in charge of the manufacture of gunpowder for the government in the years before the French Revolution. At that time in America there was a great demand for gunpowder. It was needed for all sorts of excavation, such as road and canal building, as well as for hunting, which was then an important occupation.

During the Revolutionary War, George Washington had imported powder from France. The American mills were producing an inferior powder, and soon after the war many of them closed. Du Pont realized that powder making—the French way—would be a very profitable business in America. After he estimated that $36,000 would build the biggest and best powder plant in the United States, he went back to France to raise the money and purchase equipment. As the site of his future factory, he had already selected a tract of land outside Wilmington, Delaware, along the Brandywine River.

The Brandywine is a small but powerful stream that runs through granite hills toward the sea. Dropping 125 feet in its last 5 miles, it was an ideal source of power to turn the waterwheels of mill industries. When Irénée Du Pont came along, mills along the Brandywine were already grinding corn and wheat into flour, producing paper and cotton cloth, sawing lumber and making iron hardware. He purchased a site that had previously been used by a cotton miller, and soon began work on the many buildings of his company, called Eleutherian Mills.

He had been in business for two years when a Wilmington newspaper printed a grocer's advertisement of products including "Dupont & Co's Gunpowder, superior to any imported." As Du Pont's business expanded, he acquired additional property in the Hagley area a bit downstream, and in 1814 joined with other businessmen to build a textile mill.

The Du Pont Company is today the world's largest chemical manufacturer, and about a third of its total production is synthetic fibers such as nylon. The Hagley Museum, located in some of the earliest Du Pont buildings, tells the story of the company's growth and of developing American industry.

Your visit could begin at the old textile mill, which on the outside still looks the same as it did more than 150 years ago. Exhibits on the first floor trace the history of the Brandywine region, beginning with the time when only the Delaware Indians lived along its banks. Sharpening stones by striking other stones against them,

Lavoisier and young Du Pont

grinding corn and nuts by hand, the Indians never dreamed that the nearby waters could make their work easier. In the seventeenth century, Swedish settlers harnessed the rushing Brandywine. It was the Swedes who brought the waterwheel into the region. A model of a small flour mill built of logs shows another Swedish contribution—the basic log cabin construction.

In Revolutionary days Wilmington was the nation's flour-milling center. The rich farmlands of New Jersey, Pennsylvania, Delaware and Maryland grew most of America's wheat in the years before the frontier was pushed westward. A particularly inventive Wilmington millwright, Oliver Evans, developed an automatic flour mill. In a model of it you can see chutes carrying the partly milled flour down one floor to the next operation.

Other displays tell of the arrival of the Du Pont family, and one shows young Irénée learning the chemistry of gunpowder in the laboratory of his master, Lavoisier.

On the second floor you can see exhibits that carry the story of American industry through mass production, the assembly line and other developments. When you come back down, you can take

53

Exhibit shows flour milling in early America. Wheat is raised to the upper loft of the mill, where it is screened and cleaned, then channeled to millstones for grinding. In a bolting or sifting machine it is graded into fine and coarse flour for barreling and shipment.

the little bus that comes by about every half hour. In it you can ride for a mile and a half along the Brandywine to see other buildings and exhibits related to the Du Pont family and company.

Several buildings are small and square with steeply slanting roofs. These are the old stone mills. Usually, two were built close together, with a large shared mill wheel between them. Three sides of each mill are sturdily constructed. The fourth side, facing the river, is intentionally flimsy. If there were an explosion, it would blow out this light side, in a direction away from the houses where the workers or the Du Ponts lived.

After a few minutes the bus stops at the Black Powder Exhibit Building. Here you can see every step in the manufacture of gunpowder as it was produced in the Du Pont mills.

Only three ingredients are necessary to make explosive powder: saltpeter, sulfur and charcoal. Irénée Du Pont imported from India most of his saltpeter—the common name for the chemical compound potassium nitrate. His sulfur came from Italy. In what was called the charcoal house, charred remnants of burned willow were ground powder-fine.

The most dangerous step in the process was known as incorporation. This was the stage at which the three ingredients were mixed together. There is a model of a mill in which huge cast-iron wheels move over the powdered ingredients, mixing and mixing until the product becomes uniform. A workman pours water on the powder under the wheels. In this way he cools the ingredients and reduces the danger of explosion touched off by heat generated by the rolling wheels.

Another model shows the press house where the damp mixture was dried and blended further in a hand-turned screw press. There is a model of the graining mill in which screens separated different-sized grains of black powder. (Coarser powder was for cannon and construction blasting; finer powder for small arms.) In the dry house, powder on trays along the walls was dried by heat from a

55

Saltpeter refinery

Press house

Powder magazine

stove (or, in good weather, on long tables in the sun). In the glazing mill the powder was tumbled for hours in huge wooden barrels. This continued the drying process and rounded the grains so that they would pour easily.

Near the mills was the shop of the cooper who made barrels or kegs for the powder; the 25-pound size was standard, but other sizes were also made. The building where powder was stored for shipment was called the magazine. Workers here wore wrappings around their feet to reduce friction when they walked. It took very little to set off an explosion, and for this reason the magazine was at a distance from the mills.

57

Stone mill houses

The last scene in the Black Powder Exhibit shows kegs being unloaded from a Conestoga wagon and taken onto a ship. After you've seen it and come out of this building, the bus driver will show you the two 10-ton cast-iron rolling wheels that are still in one of the incorporation mills at the river's edge nearby.

The bus goes on to the home where Irénée Du Pont and his family and descendants lived. You can also visit the small office from which Irénée's son, Alfred Victor, carried on the business and, near it, the big barn that housed the horses and wagons of the company. The barn was also the center of the farm that provided most of the food for the men who worked the mills. A library has recently been built near the barn, and in it are the records of the Du Pont Company dating back to its beginnings in 1802.

Part II
ART

8

WILLIAM ROCKHILL NELSON
GALLERY OF ART
AND THE ATKINS MUSEUM
OF FINE ARTS
4525 Oak Street
Kansas City, Missouri 64111

How does an art museum get started? Here's how it happened in Kansas City.

When newspaper publisher William Rockhill Nelson came to Kansas City in 1880, the streets were muddy and unpaved; the houses were uninviting. He looked around and decided that it was an ugly place in which to live. Yet he had a job to do here and he wanted to stay. He decided that the town must be made over.

61

William Rockhill Nelson

Making over a town is no easy matter. But as founder of an influential newspaper, the Kansas City *Star,* Nelson was in a good position to gain support for his cause. He pleaded so strongly for civic improvement that the town roused itself and raised enough money over a period of time to build parks, bridges, paved roads and better buildings.

In those years thousands of prosperous Americans took what was called the grand tour of Europe—a long and luxurious trip that might last several months or even years. William Rockhill Nelson's turn came in the 1890's, and the paintings and sculptures he saw in museums and mansions everywhere he went filled him with both delight and envy. There was nothing like this at home. Only in New York, whose Metropolitan Museum of Art was just twenty years old, and where millionaires competed with one another in building elegant homes along Fifth Avenue, had he seen such paintings. But in his hometown—indeed, in the entire middle of the nation—there was absolutely none.

62

Once he had an idea in his head, Mr. Nelson was always quick to act on it. From a European dealer he bought nineteen copies that had been made of famous Italian and Dutch paintings. He shipped them off to Kansas City, where they were displayed in the basement of the public library.

But Nelson realized that this was only a beginning. So he drew up a will in which he left most of his fortune to the city for a really good museum. Years later, another local art lover, Mary Atkins, decided to add a large sum of her own to Nelson's legacy, and the museum that resulted bears both their names.

While the museum building was going up, a committee of art experts was chosen by the city to go shopping in Europe. They had more than $1,000,000 to spend. A million is a substantial sum even now, but in 1930 it could buy a great deal more than it does today. The art experts came back with some very choice paintings, including a well-known portrait by Goya and a famous painting by Jean Baptiste Chardin, "The Soap Bubble Blowers." (If you

have visited New York's Metropolitan or Washington's National Gallery, you may have seen other, slightly different versions of this painting. Chardin, who lived in France during the eighteenth century, did many pictures of children at play.)

Twenty years after the arrival of "The Soap Bubble Blowers," the museum had another benefactor. He was Samuel H. Kress, who had made a fortune from a chain of five-and-ten-cent stores throughout the country. He too took a grand tour of Europe, and decided to become an art collector when he saw a group of masterpieces in the villa of an Italian count. Kress was a man of frugal habits. The purchase of fine paintings and sculpture became the one luxury which he allowed himself. After several years he had so many works of art that he would have built a museum of his own in New York. But he was talked into giving everything to the new National Gallery in Washington. Even after that, Kress kept buying. Soon there were enough great paintings in Washington for the collection to be divided into several parts. One part stayed there; the others went to eighteen cities whose Kress Stores had helped make their owner wealthy. Kansas City was one of the eighteen.

In the gallery where works of the early Italian Renaissance given by Kress are on display are two wooden statues, one of the Virgin Mary, one of the Archangel Gabriel. No one knows the name of the sculptor who carved them out of wood in Florence. But there are still traces of the colors he painted on them, and the angel still wears the metal wings given him some 600 years ago.

There are other Kress gifts here whose creators are not known by name today. Art detectives are at work trying to track them down.

All sleuths depend on clues, and painters leave many behind. In the "Portrait of a Young Lady," for example, the most important clue was the unusual amount of jewelry worn by the model. Her lace hairnet is covered with jeweled flowers; she wears an elaborate necklace and a pin in the shape of a lion's head; and her cape, which has slipped off her shoulders, is held by a heavy chain with a large jeweled clasp in the shape of scorpions.

The detectives searched for other paintings of young women wearing elaborate jewelry. They found two portraits. In both of these, as in the Nelson Gallery "Portrait," there was a resemblance to the work of Leonardo da Vinci, particularly in the delicacy of the face. One artist—perhaps a student of Leonardo's—might have painted all three portraits.

X-rays of the Nelson Gallery portrait were taken. Under the paint was a simple first sketch of the face, without the jewelry or the embroidery on the cape that appear on the finished canvas. Perhaps the great Leonardo himself made the preliminary drawing, and then turned the work over to a pupil who completed it. This was customary when an artist had so many orders that he could not personally fill them all. That Leonardo let his advanced students help in this way was proved by the discovery of a letter written in 1501 by a monk who visited his studio and described how he worked with his pupils.

Also in the Nelson Gallery is a "Portrait of a Young Man" thought to have been sketched by Leonardo but completed by a different pupil.

The Nelson Gallery has a rich variety of collections. If you are interested in the arts of India and China, the Oriental rooms are for you. If you like ceramics and silver from England, you can find fine examples of these. Another room is devoted to Missouri's George Caleb Bingham who painted portraits of Missourians as well as scenes of daily life at the middle of the last century. Bingham was a politician as well as a painter. He was elected to the state legislature and also served as state treasurer and president of the Kansas City Board of Police Commissioners. "Canvassing for a Vote" pictures a moment he was very familiar with—the politician stopping for what he hopes will be a persuasive chat with possible supporters.

Because he painted what was familiar to his contemporaries,

"Canvassing for a Vote"

Bingham's works were popular. Engravings made from them hung in many farmhouses. "Canvassing for a Vote" was, in fact, known only from these engravings. The original painting had been sent to Paris to be reproduced, and although the prints came back, the painting did not. For almost 100 years it was believed lost. It was rediscovered only when its last owner, hearing of the large collection of Binghams in Kansas City, wrote to the Nelson Gallery about it. He later sold it to them.

9

WHITNEY MUSEUM OF AMERICAN ART
946 Madison Avenue
New York, New York 10021

"SEA SENTINEL" BY THEODORE ROSZAK

The Whitney is the place to see—and to feel—what America looks like to its artists. It has the most complete collection of twentieth-century American art of any museum in the country.

Here you will see art inspired by factories, crowded beaches, neon lights, cereal-box tops, skyscrapers, subways, small-town streets in their Sunday morning emptiness, field hands and office-workers. Exactly what you see depends on when you happen to visit, for the exhibits change from month to month.

The first time you come it is hard to do more than form a general impression. The building itself may surprise you. You may find it stark, bare, strange; or perhaps massive, simple, beautiful! The windows are irregularly placed. Architects Marcel Breuer and Hamilton Smith have used windows to form a sculptural design on the outside rather than to light the interior.

Inside the building you find that the elevators are unexpectedly big and tall. They must carry very large paintings and sculptures. If you go straight up to the fourth floor, you will step off the elevator into an enormous open space with a very high ceiling. There is a window that may take you by surprise when you get to it, for it suddenly brings you into sharp contact with the street outside.

In this room you will probably find very large canvases in intense colors and pieces of sculpture in shining metal or plastic. These are impressions of today's world by today's artists. Compare your reactions to them with the feelings you get from today's music.

In contrast, John Steuart Curry's "Baptism in Kansas" shows a

scene of American rural life in the 1920's. Here on a Kansas farm, a country preacher is about to immerse a rapt young woman, the first of a group of seven, while the neighboring farmers, dressed in their Sunday clothes, sing hymns.

Grant Wood's "Dinner for Threshers" takes you inside a farmhouse to show you more of farm life. And Thomas Hart Benton gives you close-ups of rural faces. Edward Hopper's "Early Sunday Morning, Seven A.M." and "Second Story Sunlight" take you into the small town or the outskirts of the bigger town. Perhaps you have seen Hopper's America where time seems to stand still and people go nowhere. Charles Burchfield's painting "Old House by Creek" shows a decaying part of an industrial town. The city itself comes closer in Charles Dumuth's portrait of a coal elevator, "My Egypt"; an industrial scene by Charles Sheeler, "River Rouge Plant"; and a painting of "Brooklyn Bridge" by Joseph Stella.

In the 1930's, a period well represented at the Whitney, America was going through the Depression. Jobs were scarce and people were starving. Then, just as now, artists spoke out about what they felt was wrong with their country. Isaac Soyer, John Sloan and Ben Shahn are only three of the artists who either recorded America's unhappiness or criticized what they thought were its causes.

Reginald Marsh and Moses and Raphael Soyer, each in his own way, found a kind of beauty in the poorer people of the big city. It is interesting to compare Marsh's painting of the subway, done in 1930, with George Tooker's version done in 1950. Marsh shows the inside of a train late at night. It is dirty; the people seem exhausted. Tooker is concerned only with the station, which he turns into the setting for a nightmare. It is clean and brightly lit. The travelers in the station appear tense, lost and locked in.

There is tremendous joy and exhilaration in city life also. These are the qualities caught in the vivid abstractions of Stuart Davis and the "Manhattan Skyscrapers" of Lyonel Feininger.

In addition to its paintings, the Whitney has an excellent collec-

"Sacrifice II"

tion of sculpture that can be found placed here and there indoors or in the garden at the front of the museum. Jacques Lipchitz's "Sacrifice II" re-creates, larger and more beautiful than life, a scene out of the past of the Jewish people. Having rejected the ritual of human sacrifice, the Jews gave instead the lives of animals as a sign of their awe of God.

And then there is William Zorach's marble sculpture of "The Future Generation." It shows a proud mother and her handsome little boy looking ahead with confidence and hope.

Some of the pieces displayed in the sculpture gallery may make you think twice about what sculpture is. Many of today's sculptors do not limit themselves to clay, bronze and stone, the materials with which sculptors have most often worked. Today's sculptors work with the materials of everyday living—painted wood, scrap metal from old automobiles, clear plastic, white plaster, scraps of

70

fabric and neon lights. Edward Keinholtz has put together a highly theatrical work that looks like a moment from an eerie play frozen for all time. He has re-created a corner of an old-fashioned room which suggests that people are still living there, but are dead to what is going on in the world outside. Life-size white plaster figures by George Segal are ghostlike replicas of very real people. And you are sure to find something by Alexander Calder, the originator of the mobile. The word "mobile" means "able to move," and Calder's most famous sculptures do just that. He cut free-form shapes out of heavy sheetmetal, and colored them brightly in red, white, black. Then he balanced them—carefully, with scientific precision—on slender wire arms. The slightest motion of the air will set these shapes gliding. Calder has created a sculpture with a form which is always changing.

Whitney Museum Sculpture Gallery

After he had been making mobiles for many years, Calder created another kind of sculpture that he called a stabile. This word means "standing still." These new pieces are large, black, jagged shapes of heavy metal. They are fixed in position—but they too are always changing. However, you have to move around a stabile to see it change. Bend down low and look up at it; look up through it; look into it. The Whitney usually displays a Calder stabile in its outdoor sculpture gallery below street level. You can look down at it as you leave the museum.

Sculpture is particularly at home in this museum whose founder was a sculptress. Mrs. Gertrude Vanderbilt Whitney began welcoming artists into her Greenwich Village studio in the early part of the century. And little by little, she grew determined to start a museum.

72

10

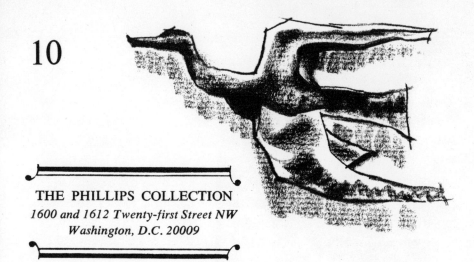

The house on Twenty-first Street in northwest Washington belonged to very rich people and it is much bigger than the houses most of us live in, but it has the feeling of a familiar place. Both outside and in all its many rooms, it makes one feel that it is a home rather than a museum. At the Phillips house you can sit on the sofas and chairs and relax in the presence of art masterpieces.

You can begin with "The Round Table" by Georges Braque. Braque set out to rearrange the visible world in his art. He said, "We must not imitate what we want to create." He would create something new, something more than the real object that was his starting point. And his new creation would follow its own natural laws.

Braque wanted his painting of a table to show more than anyone's eye could see of it at one time; he wanted to show the part of the table that you know is there even though it is hidden from you, as well as the part you can see from where you are standing. To show all of the table, he flattened it out as one might flatten a cardboard box. When the table is flat, a pattern emerges that is made up of its recognizable shapes, but now they are in a new relationship to one another. The pattern of the table blends with

73

"The Round Table"

the pattern of the things that are on it, and with the pattern of the floor and the wall.

In another painting by Braque called "The Wash Stand" you can again find objects broken up and reassembled in a new relationship that is at once familiar and strange.

A large canvas called "Interior with Egyptian Curtain" was completed by Henri Matisse in 1948 when he was seventy-nine years old. It is related to, but different from, the Braques. The colors in this painting are vibrant. The pattern is an arrangement of rectangles. Although the pattern was more important to the artist than the objects, the objects are still recognizable.

Near it is a work by the Dutch artist Piet Mondrian, who was not concerned with objects at all. He was interested only in patterns. His patterns are made up of rectangles, some filled with primary colors. But the shapes and colors are arranged in such perfect balance that you can't imagine changing a line of it without destroying the whole.

"Ochre and Red on Red" is the name of a very large unframed painting by the American Mark Rothko. Rothko was not concerned with objects either. He was interested in the effects of colors on one another. On his canvas a big, fuzzily outlined rectangle of ochre (a yellowish-brown earth color) and another of red are set against a background of a different shade of red. You have to peer at it for a while to see where the background begins and the rectangles within it end. Rothko's colors change one another—his ochre looks different in the middle of its rectangle from the way it looks at the edges, where it meets the background red. This artist's colors also change *you*; when you stand in front of this painting, your face looks orange. You are a part of the painting while you are looking at it.

About 100 years ago, a group of artists who were also concerned with colors and how they change were working in France. One of them, Pierre Auguste Renoir, painted "The Luncheon of the Boating Party," which is probably the most famous painting in the Phillips Collection.

Renoir and many of his friends became known as Impressionists. They noticed that the colors of real things seem to change from hour to hour as the sun changes its position. In their paintings they tried to show the effect, or impression, of light on whatever subjects they chose. With short brush strokes, they applied colors to their canvases, arranged very carefully, so that the viewer's eye could blend them.

"The Luncheon of the Boating Party" is a painting full of sunshine, sunshine so bright you can almost feel it. But Renoir did not paint the sun. Instead, he showed the white of blouses and tablecloths, the yellow of straw hats, the glisten of bottles and glasses and fresh fruit as they look when the sun shines on them. You know the sun is there, even though you don't see it in the painting. If you look closely at the canvas, you will see the individual brush strokes of pinks, blues and yellows that Renoir figured out he had to use to show how white a white tablecloth can be in brightest noonday light.

Marjorie and Duncan Phillips loved their collection dearly. They loved their home too. And when their collection needed more space than the house comfortably provided, they were faced with a problem. How could they add enough space for the works of art, and still keep the feeling of the home that Mr. Phillips had grown up in ? They solved it in an ingenious way. A very modern-looking, box-shaped building was put up on the other side of the driveway. It forms the main entrance to the museum. Upstairs, two glass-walled passageways cross over the driveway, leading from the second and third floors of this new wing into the older building. And even in the modern new section, chairs and sofas and room-size galleries make you feel comfortably at home.

In their art collection, too, Mr. and Mrs. Phillips tried to show how comfortably modern art and earlier works could blend. Among the earlier works are two paintings of the repentant Peter from the Bible. One comes from the seventeenth century and is by El Greco. The other, from the nineteenth century, is by Goya.

The display of art at the Phillips Collection changes frequently and it is just possible that one of the paintings we have talked about may not be exhibited when you visit. But you can easily enough find a substitute. Among the Impressionists you can choose from are Degas and Monet. The largest group of works by Bonnard in America is here. Earlier French artists whose work paved the way for the Impressionists are Corot and Courbet. Among the modern Americans are John Marin, Karl Knaths, Arthur Dove and Milton Avery, a group of men to whom Marjorie and Duncan Phillips were friends as well as patrons.

11

Art is a clue to the customs of the people who produce it. A wooden mask from Africa, a stone head from ancient Mexico, a feathered headdress from Peru and a carved stone wall from an Assyrian palace are the kinds of clues anthropologists have studied for years. But the Brooklyn Museum pioneered in displaying these objects for their own sake; for their beauty, for their ability to please or astound.

Mexican stone head

Peruvian hat

When you go to the Brooklyn Museum, you will see a great mask made by the Baga tribe of French Guinea. It was carved by an artist for the purpose—so the artist and his friends believed—of helping women have babies.

The mask represents a goddess of fertility and maternity. It is carved of wood and is hollow so that it can be worn over the head of a dancer. The mask comes all the way down and rests on the dancer's shoulders. It consists of the head, shoulders and breast of the goddess. The top of the mask towers above the dancer's head. There are tiny holes between the breasts through which he can see.

Notice the scars on the goddess' face. Scars were considered

Baga tribe Nimba mask

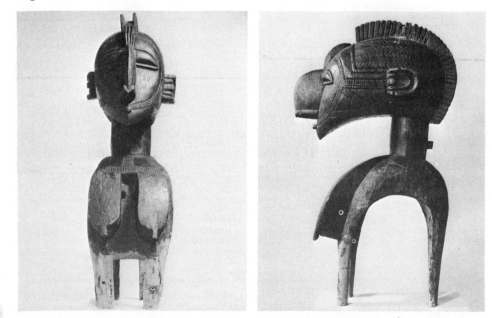

beautiful by many Africans. Each tribe had its own scar pattern for decorating the face. Young tribe members were deliberately scarred for much the same reasons that we use makeup.

Notice too how the artist divided the face into several separate areas. The geometric shapes of these areas, repeated on left and right, have a pattern and rhythm of their own. This is characteristic of other African Negro wood sculptors as well as of the Baga. This carving is a recognizable, though not quite realistic, way of representing human features. Many twentieth-century artists, among them Pablo Picasso and Jacques Lipchitz, have been influenced by African sculpture.

Not far from the Baga mask is a nail fetish carved of wood by a member of the Bakongo tribe in the Belgian Congo. He is a fierce-looking figure, and his tongue is sticking out. His eyes are made of tiny pieces of mirror which, the Bakongo believed, gave him extra power. And driven into every part of him are dozens of nails.

A fetish is an object that is believed to have magic, supernatural power. This fetish was supposed to give one the strength to overcome enemies. Each nail represents a kind of prayer. A tribesman would drive a nail into the fetish in very much the spirit in which one might light a candle in a church.

These are works of art produced by primitive societies, groups of people who have no written language. To go from the Baga mask and the Bakongo nail fetish to the art of ancient Egypt is to take a giant step away from the primitive to the work of a great civilization. Egyptian art is plentiful in the United States. Brooklyn's collection is one of the best.

But as you approach it, on the third floor of the museum, you will see large, intricately carved slabs of alabaster—a hard, whitish stone—that are not Egyptian. They date from 880 B.C. and come from the walls of the palace of King Ashurnasirpal of Assyria. A winged god is shown watering the tree of life. The container which holds the water looks almost like a lady's handbag.

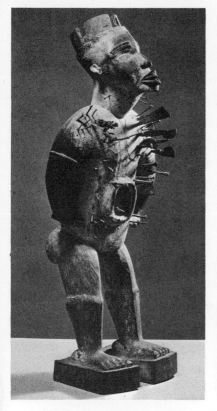

Bakongo tribe nail fetish

Assyrian winged god

Beyond the Assyrian work is the art of Egypt. Majestic, mysterious and religious, all of it tells a story of life and death. Because the Egyptians believed strongly in a life after death, we have a very complete record of their civilization. With their dead, they buried things used in daily life—pots and baskets, tools, weapons, utensils and jewelry. They believed that the soul of the dead person would need these things in the world it was about to enter. They also buried carvings of wood, ivory and bone, and clay sculptures.

Until about 3000 B.C. the Egyptian dead were buried in simple graves at the edge of the desert. Archeologists have excavated thousands of them and taken the hidden treasures to museums and universities. After 3000 B.C. graves were made larger and larger. One-room buildings with brick walls and wooden roofs were built. Later these developed into tombs that were strong as fortresses,

81

with inner rooms and connecting passages. Tombs, made even larger to suit the taste of kings, finally became the Great Pyramids.

The Egyptians believed so completely in life after death that they mummified corpses to prevent the bodies from decaying. Then the soul could live on in an unchanged body in the next world. They decorated the walls of tombs with views of harvests and dancing girls, and scenes of hunting, fishing and feasting. They filled the tombs with prized possessions and furnishings that had belonged to the dead. Once the doors were sealed, it was believed that life somehow continued for the body as well as the soul.

The Egyptians had very definite ideas about the afterlife. These are shown in colorful paintings on mummy cases or coffins. In the Brooklyn Museum are several. It is easy to find the case that covered a female mummy. It is painted to show the dead woman's wig, eye makeup and jewelry, and it is smaller and lighter-skinned than the mummy cases for men. Among the scenes of the soul's afterlife painted on the woman's case is one showing the god Osiris sitting in final judgment of her soul. The center of the scene is a giant scale. On it the goddess of truth and justice, Maat, is weighing the heart of the dead woman. Weighed against it is a feather. If the heart is heavier than the feather, it will be thrown to a waiting monster, part lion and part crocodile, and the soul will not be granted eternal happiness. A group of judges is looking on.

Another word for coffin is sarcophagus. The Brooklyn Museum has a magnificent one used for the burial of a sacred bird. Made of

wood and covered with gold leaf, it is in the shape of the ibis, a storklike bird which the Egyptians worshiped. The feet and head of the bird are silver. It is seated, its legs parallel to its body. All this makes a pleasing design. The downward curve of its beak is repeated in the curve of its feet.

Across the room from the ibis is a sacred cat, carved of wood, from the period between 600 and 300 B.C. Notice how this regal figure appears to be complete as a design even though the artist never bothered to finish the animal's two rear legs.

In the next gallery, a colossal royal head from a statue at least twice life size deserves to be looked at from every angle. This head of a young man in a battle helmet is polished stone. In the center of the helmet the sculptor placed a cobra, to spit poison at the young king's enemies. Part of the cobra has been broken off, but the part that is still there makes it easy to imagine how fearsome it must have looked.

83

Dutch Colonial house—kitchen-dining-living room

You can go from Egypt to seventeenth-century New York by traveling up to the fourth floor. Here you will find a whole Dutch Colonial house that once stood in a Brooklyn field. It was moved to the museum piece by piece only a few years ago. You can't go inside it, but you can walk all around it and look in through its low windows. It has two rooms. The north room served as a parlor-bedroom. The beds are concealed behind curtains in separate, closetlike enclosures, called bed boxes, against one wall. Against another wall is an odd-looking machine that might easily be an instrument of torture. It is a napkin press, used to flatten and smooth cloth napkins just as you might by ironing them.

You may want to stop at the gift shop on your way out. It's one of the best museum gift shops in the country.

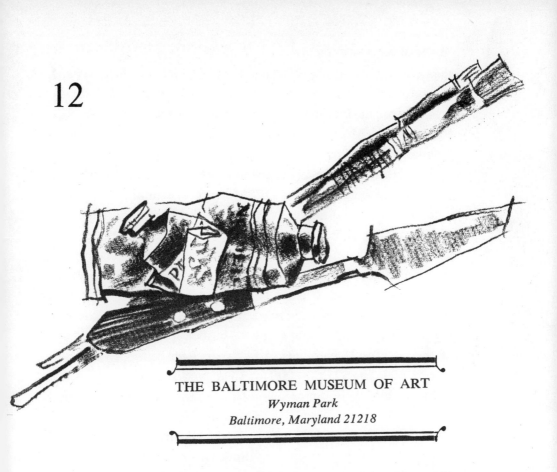

12

THE BALTIMORE MUSEUM OF ART
Wyman Park
Baltimore, Maryland 21218

In the early years of the twentieth century several American millionaires seemed determined to outdo one another in finding ways to spend their money. Their extravagances were reported on the front pages of newspapers all over the country. They built mansions on New York's Fifth Avenue, summer homes in Newport, Rhode Island, and winter homes in Florida. They bought furniture for these homes in Europe. Even the wood paneling for walls and ceilings, the marble for floors and entrances, came from the Old World. And, to decorate their paneled walls, they bought paintings by famous European artists. Eventually most of their furnishings and works of art went into museums. Even their homes sometimes became museums.

J. P. Morgan was perhaps the most extravagant, and probably

the richest, of this group. His New York mansion, in which he kept his thousands of rare books, priceless manuscripts and fine drawings, became the Pierpont Morgan Library. He was a generous contributor to the Metropolitan Museum of Art, and was its president for many years. After he died, 6,000 of his paintings, sculptures, pieces of furniture, porcelain and other objects went to the Metropolitan—and this was only half the Morgan collection!

There was also Andrew W. Mellon, who started the National Gallery of Art in Washington, D.C., by presenting to the nation about 150 works of art and a large marble building. Worth about $50,000,000, this was the largest gift ever made to any government by one person. It is the only national art museum that was privately initiated and endowed. Compared to Morgan, Mellon lived quietly, but he bought art by the bushel, spending $7,000,000 at one time for 21 paintings. A few years later he topped his own record, spending $21,000,000 for 42 art works.

Meanwhile, in Baltimore, without any fanfare, two wealthy sisters were living with a growing collection of modern art. The elder, Dr. Claribel Cone, had entered medical school in 1900. After graduating, she went to Europe to continue her research. Her traveling companion was her sister, Miss Etta.

In Paris friends introduced the sisters to the artist Henri Matisse. He was the leader of a group known as *les fauves*—the wild beasts —because of the vibrant colors and unexpected design of their work. The Cones visited his studio, and bought a painting. That was the beginning of a collection of Matisses that, when it later went to the Baltimore Museum, consisted of 42 paintings, 18 bronze sculptures, and 113 drawings.

The most famous Matisse in Baltimore is "The Blue Nude." The distorted outline of this reclining figure was considered scandalous at the time the Cones bought it. To many it seemed that the artist had painted a woman with a dislocated hip. But Matisse had simply used the female form to create a rhythmic design. A bronze "Reclining Nude" in almost the same position is his sculptured equivalent of the painting.

The Cone sisters met Pablo Picasso when he was just beginning the work that would make him the most famous artist of the twentieth century. He told them that he liked to read the comics in American newspapers. So Dr. Claribel and Miss Etta cut them out of the newspapers from home and saved them. When they visited Picasso's studio, they brought him big bundles of them. While the artist read them, the sisters browsed around, looking at his sketches and drawings and choosing some to buy for themselves.

Picasso had been born in Spain. His father, Don José, was a painting teacher, and from the time Pablo entered school he could draw. The other children invented a game to test him. They would ask him to draw something—a dog or a donkey, perhaps—starting with the ear, or the eye, or the paw. As the young artist met these challenges, his skill increased. By the time he was thirteen, his father could see that the boy would outdo him as an artist. And so the father presented to his son his own paints and brushes. A few years later Pablo won an honorable mention at the Fine Arts Exhibition in Madrid.

When Pablo Picasso met Dr. Claribel and Miss Etta, he was twenty-five years old. His Paris studio was already heaped with drawings and paintings. And he was about to create a revolution in the art world.

Picasso's revolution is called Cubism. It is a way of showing objects broken up into their basic geometric shapes. The outline of a face may be shown as a circle or oval, a nose as a triangle or rectangle. Other shapes may be added to show parts of the object hidden from the eye. The geometric forms may be repeated to give a sense of motion or distance or size. And they may be rearranged. A mouth may appear near the top of a face, or two ears on the same side of a head. The artist is not interested in repeating what our eyes show us as everyday reality.

87

Many people believe that Picasso was influenced by African Negro sculpture, which also represents objects as arrangements of basic geometric forms. It is said that the first African piece Picasso saw belonged to Matisse, who had discovered it in a shop in Paris. But Picasso was not so sure that this was the source of his new ideas about drawing. Years later, he said, "When we invented Cubism, we had no idea that we were creating it, but we were only trying to express what we felt inside us."

Mostly the Cones bought Picasso's very early works. But even one of the earliest, "Woman with Bangs," gives a hint of the direction the artist would soon take. It is a portrait of a forlorn-looking woman. Her shoulders, neck and head are slightly distorted or stretched in an unnatural way. Somehow this distortion seems to make her even more forlorn. Her eyes, however, are drawn as sharp, deep-set ovals. They are like the eyes one sees in much African sculpture. Picasso would paint eyes like these many times.

A few years later he was working on "The Young Ladies of Avignon," the painting that would announce his Cubist revolution. (You can see it at the Museum of Modern Art in New York.) Before painting its five figures, he made many drawings. One of these, a "Nude with Raised Arm," was bought by the Cones. The face is an elongated oval, with a sharply angled nose slashing across it. The legs and torso have been broken up into basic shapes, almost as if they were made of curved and angled building blocks, and these shapes are repeated so that the young woman seems to be walking.

Although Dr. Claribel died in 1927, Miss Etta went on adding to their collection for twenty years. Every year on Matisse's birthday she sent him a telegram of congratulations, and almost every year she bought another of his paintings. But she also decided to go back in time and round out the Cone Collection with French art of the nineteenth century. A painting that once hung in a corner of her living room is Paul Gauguin's "Woman with Mango,"

"Woman with Mango"

one of many done during the artist's years on the island of Tahiti.

When Miss Etta died, she left the collection to the Baltimore Museum. Other Baltimore collectors have added art from other periods and other places. The museum has received gifts of old masters, including Titian, Van Dyck and Rembrandt, as well as gifts of magnificent works by unknown African, Oriental and pre-Columbian artists.

In the museum's Maryland Wing are four fully furnished eighteenth-century rooms. Settlers raised tobacco on their large plantations, and exported it in their ships, becoming wealthy merchants. Their finest furniture, silver and family portraits are now here.

But on your first visit, you may want to spend all your time among the paintings. There's enough beauty and excitement in them to hold you for hours.

Comic strip from Baltimore American, *1911*

13

THE TOLEDO MUSEUM OF ART
Monroe Street at Scottwood Avenue
Toledo, Ohio 43601

Toledo's museum is especially known for its superb collections of glass and books. To understand why such seemingly ordinary objects belong in an art museum, you must remember that only within the last 200 years have glass and books been common enough for everyday use. For most of the several thousand years since glass and books were first made, only the richest people, such as kings and priests, could afford them. And like many other things intended for the use and pleasure of a privileged few, these were made by hand and made as beautifully as possible.

The story of glass probably begins with a prehistoric campfire built on sandy soil. When the fire died down, a clear and glistening

Eastern Mediterranean sand-core ware

substance may have been discovered in the firebed. Perhaps the men who found it passed it from hand to hand, wondering what it might be; perhaps one of them tried to bend it and it broke.

Centuries of experimentation followed, and by 2000 B.C. Egyptian craftsmen were quite skilled at molding glass around a shape or core, usually made of copper. After the molten glass cooled and hardened, the core could be removed. The copper gave a dark blue color to their jars and vials, bowls and vases, beads and figurines.

The next great glassmakers were the ancient Romans. By their time the blowpipe had been invented. It worked something like a long bubble pipe, with a blob of hot, almost liquid glass on the far end instead of soapy water. The Romans figured out a way to blow jars from two differently colored layers of glass. Then they carved a design through the top layer, so that the bottom color showed. Many very old pieces from Egypt and Rome have a sort of

92

rainbow shimmering over the surface. This iridescence, which is often very beautiful, was not put there by the original glassmaker; he never even saw it. It was caused by chemical changes during the centuries the glass lay buried in the earth.

Glass was America's first industry. The settlers at Jamestown had a factory going within a year after the colony was founded. The raw materials—sand, and wood for fuel—were easily located. The Jamestown factory made beads for trading with the Indians, and goblets and vases to send back to be sold in England.

With the arrival of skilled European glassmakers, the young nation's glass industry flourished. Factories were established in Pennsylvania, New Jersey, Maryland, New York, Massachusetts and Ohio. Improved manufacturing techniques made windowpanes and bottles available to almost everyone. At the same time new ways of coloring and ornamenting were found, and artisans still took pride in turning out unusual and decorative pieces. Look at the jewellike blues and ambers and amethysts of the tumblers and bowls on display at the museum, the designs engraved on or cut into decanters and lamp bases, and gracefully shaped jars and bottles. This glass belongs in an art museum.

Toledo's Gallery of the Book is devoted to the history of the written and printed word, from the beginning of man's attempts to communicate in writing. The earliest writings do not look very much like books. The Nebuchadnezzar Cylinder belonged to the King of Babylon about 2,500 years ago. It looks more like a vase than like any kind of book we're accustomed to. It is, in fact, made of clay. There was no paper in those days. To write on the clay, a wedge-shaped tool was pressed into the surface of the cylinder while the clay was still soft. Then the "book" was dried and baked

Cylinder seal of Nebuchadnezzar

Page from 1450 manuscript, Coronation of the Virgin

in the sun until it hardened. This kind of writing, in which various combinations of wedges represent words, is called cuneiform.

The picture writing of the ancient Egyptians is called hieroglyphics. A stone slab more than 4,200 years old has colorful and intricate pictures that were carved and painted on its surface after it was covered with a layer of plaster.

Illuminated manuscripts were produced in Europe before there were printing presses. A man would spend days decorating just one page of a hand-lettered book. Elaborate ornaments of gold and gleaming reds, blues, greens and yellows were painted in the margins and around initial letters, between paragraphs and sometimes all over a page.

About 500 years ago, a German printer, Johann Gutenberg, invented movable type. A page from his first book, the Gutenberg Bible, is in Toledo. A quarter of a century later, William Caxton became the first printer in England. In 1481 he produced the first English language book with illustrations. Called *Myrrour of the Worlde*, it is a sort of encyclopedia. It, too, is here.

Page from Myrrour of the Worlde

The first book published in America is also here. It was written by John Eliot, minister of a church in Roxbury, Massachusetts. He decided to learn the language of a nearby group of Indians in order to teach them Christianity. Their language had never had a written form, so he first had to invent a way of writing it. Then he translated the Bible—both the Old and the New Testaments—into their Algonquian language. The work was printed in Cambridge in 1661. The next step was for Eliot to teach the Indians how to read their own language.

The founder of the Toledo Museum of Art was Edward Drummond Libbey, who also founded the Libbey Glass Company, one of the city's major industries. The museum's glass collection was begun by Libbey himself, and many unusual pieces from his factory are included. Among them is a great punch bowl of clear cut glass that was made for display at the St. Louis World's Fair of 1904.

Libbey also bought many of the Spanish paintings for which the museum is well known. The "Man with Wine Glass" by Diego Velásquez must have been a particular favorite of Libbey, who manufactured wineglasses by the thousands.

Whenever possible, the paintings are shown with furniture and other art objects from the same time and place. So, in the seventeenth-century Dutch gallery, you will find Delft plates and vases, carved tables and chairs and a wonderful cabinet of carved oak inlaid with ebony—a setting just right for the Dutch paintings. Look for "The Flute Player" by Frans Hals here. The face glows as if a light from an invisible source were shining directly onto it.

Libbey bought mostly works of the German, Dutch and Spanish schools, and ended with works of the nineteenth century. But the museum's collection has grown to include paintings from Italy, France, England and America of the same period, and new works from our own day as well.

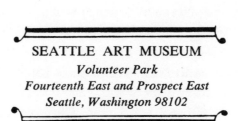

14

SEATTLE ART MUSEUM
Volunteer Park
Fourteenth East and Prospect East
Seattle, Washington 98102

If the large marble camels at the entrance to the Seattle Art Museum could talk, they would have a thrilling tale to tell you. They were carved in China in the early fifteenth century, and placed in front of the tomb of Prince Kao Sui of the Ming Dynasty. Statues of animals and warriors, utensils made of bronze and porcelain and other symbols of wealth and high position were customarily buried with Chinese royalty so that the dead man would have suitably rich possessions with him when he arrived in the next world. Five hundred years later these camels, and the lions, rams and tigers that you can see nearby, were carefully wrapped and loaded onto a ship that took them across the Pacific Ocean. Somehow—no one seems quite sure how—they were stored away in the warehouse of

Gump's Department Store in San Francisco. When they were discovered ten years later, still in their wrappings, the director of Seattle's museum heard of them. He lost no time in adding them to his collection of Oriental art, now so large that only about 10 percent of it can be shown at a time.

Among the fine pieces in this collection is a statue of the Chinese goddess of mercy, who assists Buddha in bringing spiritual salvation to man. Her name is Kuan Yin, which means "being who observes the world." She was carved 900 years ago from a single piece of wood more than five feet high. The base of the statue is carved to represent the lotus, a traditional symbol of the Buddha and his disciples. A pearly-white flower that grows in muddy earth, the lotus symbolizes the purity which man must attain to reach nirvana, a state of perfection and communion with Buddha. If this Kuan Yin is not on display, look for others. Whether of wood, stone, ivory or jade, they will all be standing on the lotus flower. Buddhism is practiced throughout most of Asia. Some of the goddesses of mercy at the museum are from Japan, where she is known as Kwannon.

In seventeenth-century Japan, the rulers, called shoguns, had vast and elaborate palaces. The finest artists were hired to make luxurious furnishings for them, and the most precious materials

were used. Seattle has a screen of six silk panels completely covered with gold leaf. A flock of blackbirds in flight is painted on it. Called "The Hundred Black Crows," the screen is the work of an artist of the Kano family. For more than 200 years this family did paintings on silk, and was particularly famous for screens such as this one. Young artists would come to study with the Kano masters, serving a sort of apprenticeship. The most promising of them were adopted and given the family name. This was according to a Japanese tradition that was followed in almost every art and craft in which apprentices served a master.

The art of making lacquerware was uniquely developed in Japan, after being learned from the Chinese. Seattle has a very early example, a thin bowl of red and black, painted with graceful animal and bird forms.

Lacquer is a very hard varnish made from the sap of the lac tree, an Asian sumac. A lacquer bowl started taking shape after a base of very thin white pine was made and covered with fine silk. The craftsman rubbed the silk until it was smooth and tight. Then he began to apply clear lacquer, layer by layer. As each coat dried, he rubbed and polished the bowl again. After there were many layers of lacquer, he painted in the designs. Then more layers of lacquer were added, and each was rubbed and polished. This bowl shines

as though it were made of glass; yet it is as thin and light as a fine teacup.

Sometimes gold dust was dropped onto the still-wet lacquer, or bits of mother-of-pearl were pressed into it, to make the design. Seattle has a writing box with a design of tree trunks and cranes outlined in gold against a brownish-black background. Pewter and lead have been inlaid, or set into the lacquer, giving parts of the design a rough texture.

Jade is a rare stone found in parts of Asia. The Chinese, who consider it a precious gem, particularly prize it for its pale, usually whitish-green color. Although it looks soft and feels smooth and waxy, it is very hard indeed. The Chinese craftsmen who worked with it, creating small sculptures and pieces of jewelry, had to use saws for cutting and iron drills for carving the details of their designs. Jade was polished with dust made from such stones as rubies, quartz, garnet and emery. This dust had the effect of sandpaper. It was rubbed on the jade with pieces of wood or leather.

Seattle has a whole gallery devoted to Chinese jade work. One of the loveliest pieces is a little "Jade Mountain," only 7¾ inches high, which despite its small size and delicate color captures the strength and majesty of a real mountain.

Ceramics is the name given to plates, vases, bowls, figurines and other things made of clay that has been baked, or fired, until it is hard. The earliest in the Seattle collection are pieces of unglazed Japanese pottery decorated only with marks that seem to have been made by pressing rope into the still-soft clay.

Much later, the Chinese discovered a pale greenish-white glaze, or glass-like coating, for their wares. Possibly this glaze, called celadon, was an imitation of jade. The Chinese also invented porcelain, which is very thin and hard, and makes a ringing sound when you tap it with your finger. Some of the porcelains are gaily multicolored; some are in soft shades of rose or green or yellow. They

100

range in size from tiny teacups without handles to huge urns and vases.

The Japanese believed that the ideal woman should be educated in literature and art, and excel at entertaining, writing and domestic accomplishments. The master Hokusai did a painting on silk of "Five Beauties," each a lovely woman embodying one of these five feminine virtues. This artist, now regarded as one of Japan's greatest, became famous only after he was forty-five years old. Fortunately he lived on for another forty-five years, and his

most celebrated paintings were done in the last twenty years of his life. He is best known for his woodblock prints of waterfalls, bridges, the graceful Mount Fuji, and other Japanese landscapes, and for his drawings of roly-poly wrestlers.

Hokusai once wrote, "At seventy-five I have learned a little about the structure of nature—of animals, plants and trees, birds, fishes and insects. In consequence, when I am eighty I shall have made a little more progress. At ninety I shall penetrate the mystery of things. At a hundred I shall certainly have reached a marvelous stage, and when I am a hundred and ten, everything I do—be it a line or a dot—will be alive." When he was dying, he shouted, "If heaven would only grant me ten more years, or only five, I might still become a great artist."

Seattle also has a large collection of works by American artists of our own day, especially those who come from the northwest corner of the country. Some critics see Oriental ideas in their paintings, and say the Chinese and Japanese collections in the museum influenced them.

Foremost among these artists is Mark Tobey, who has for many years been fascinated by the Far East and has visited both China and Japan, where he studied calligraphy, the art of writing. Oriental calligraphy is characterized by straight lines and sharply turned corners. It is done with a paintbrush, which makes it possible for the lines to be hair-thin or quite thick. Tobey liked to experiment with this technique applied to oils and canvas. The Seattle museum has the largest collection of his work in the country.

When Tobey took first prize at the Biennale art exhibition in Venice in 1958, he was the first American in more than fifty years to win it. He has said, "Artists learn only from other artists and from art." He has also said, "Today we have to know *both* worlds, the Western and the Oriental. The world is contracting fast. I live in Seattle because I don't like to get too far away from Eastern culture—especially the Japanese."

WADSWORTH ATHENEUM

25 Atheneum Square North
Hartford, Connecticut 06103

Four men, each very different from the others, influenced the growth of the Wadsworth Atheneum during its first hundred years.

Daniel Wadsworth, a dedicated community leader and a collector of American paintings, was the first to dream of a museum in Hartford.

J. Pierpont Morgan, a fabulously rich man, enlarged the original building and collected a wealth of objects that came here years later. The Morgan treasure-trove included 86 Egyptian, Greek and Roman statues, and more than 360 porcelain figurines made in Germany's Meissen factories in the eighteenth century.

Samuel Colt, inventor of the revolver, divided his time between manufacturing firearms and buying art. He left collections of both that are now in the museum.

And an artistic and brilliant man, A. Everett Austin, came to the Atheneum in 1927 as its director and proceeded to make the museum internationally famous.

The first thing Austin did was go shopping. He went, of course, to Europe, where he bought a kind of art of the late sixteenth century and the seventeenth known as Baroque. Because it was then not much in demand on the art market, it was considerably less expensive than the more popular works of the Renaissance period. Little by little, Austin built up one of the best Baroque collections in the United States.

Baroque painting is detailed and dramatic. There is a theatrical use of light. A bright glow lights up a face or brilliantly highlights an action. Often the painting reminds one of a splendidly costumed, lavishly produced play, with the actors frozen at a particularly exciting moment. Many of them are intricate, crowded with people and objects.

"Feast of Herod" by Lucas Cranach the Elder

Although painted some years before the Baroque period began, Tintoretto's "Hercules and Antaeus" shows many of these characteristics. It was one of the first works bought by Austin. Hercules, the strong man of Greek and Roman mythology, battles an evil giant who sets upon travelers and kills them. But Antaeus cannot be harmed as long as his feet are on the earth. In the lower part of the painting the two huge figures are surrounded by a crowd of astonished people. From above, an audience of gods and goddesses cheers Hercules on as he wrenches the mighty giant from the earth and prepares to kill him. Through the clouds a great light shines on the two battlers, as a spotlight might on two performing actors. Other Baroque masters whose works Austin bought are Caravaggio, Juan de Valdés Leal, Rubens, Poussin, Murillo, Lucas Cranach the Elder, and Pannini. There is an interesting story behind a painting by Juan de Valdés Leal called "Vanitas."

To commemorate his conversion to a life of religious contemplation, Don Miguel Mañara of Seville commissioned two paintings—before and after, so to speak. The "after" picture, which is now in York, England, shows him studying sacred books. Hartford has the "before" scene. In it a warning angel pulls back a pink curtain to reveal a scene from the Last Judgment. On a table in the foreground there is a clutter of books, flowers, candles and other mementos, the "vanities" which the don is not yet ready to give up.

A "Gallery of Cardinal Valenti Gonzaga" by Giovanni Paolo Pannini, done in 1749, is an example of Late Baroque. It shows an art museum of that day, with its masterpieces hung in every inch of wall space and even on the ceiling. Here was a perfect way for a Baroque painter to show off his skill with detail. The gallery Pannini re-created belonged to a cardinal, and later became the first collection in the Royal Museum in Copenhagen.

Austin also pioneered in the purchase of the art of his own time. It was an exciting period. All sorts of new ways of drawing and the use of paint were being tried. The first large American shows of Cubist and Surrealist artists were held in Hartford.

"Gallery of Cardinal Valenti Gonzaga"

During one trip to Europe Austin bought a work by the Dutch artist Piet Mondrian, "Composition in Blue and White." Today we look at this work, as well as others by the same artist, with a friendly sense of recognition. The commercial arts—advertising and industrial design—have made the solid blocks of white and color set off by black lines familiar to us. But thirty-five years ago, reactions were different. Austin took a long time to make up his mind before buying. He wrote to a friend: "I went to Mondrian's Paris studio and there were all those arrangements of rectangular and square forms in primary colors. They had always seemed limited in scope and meaning. But the longer I stayed, the more convinced I became that Mondrian was a true artist, intense, dedicated and on the track of enduring discoveries. I bought this picture from

106

him. It cost almost $400." Today, of course, it is worth many times that.

Austin's interests extended to the theater, and the Atheneum's auditorium in the Avery wing of the building was used for many dramatic presentations. Here George Balanchine's new dance company, which became the New York City Ballet, gave its first performance. Balanchine had been the last master of the world-famous Ballet Russe. And Austin acquired more than 150 drawings, watercolors and oil paintings of stage settings and costumes designed for the Ballet Russe by leading European artists.

The Atheneum owns the largest collection of Thomas Cole paintings in the country. Cole was an American landscape painter of the Hudson River school. Intensely romantic, his works give us back some of the mountains and rivers and streams as they were before they were spoiled by industrial man.

"Last of the Mohicans" by Thomas Cole

You can also see the many pieces of seventeenth-century American furniture which were collected, studied and, when necessary, repaired by a man named Wallace Nutting, a minister whose hobby became a serious and scholarly endeavor.

When you come to the Avery courtyard, look up at the eight-foot marble statue of "Venus Attended by Nymph and Satyr." It was done in the late sixteenth century by Pietro Francavilla, who came from northern France to study and work in Italy. He was commissioned to do thirteen statues, of which this was one, for a villa near Florence. In 1750, the Prince of Wales acquired all thirteen and shipped them to London. Somehow this one became separated from the others and was not seen again until 1919, when Venus was uncovered by an Englishman digging a rose garden. How all eight feet of her managed to get into the ground remains a mystery that adds to her charm.

Alexander Benois' costume sketch for Giselle

16

JOHN AND MABLE RINGLING
MUSEUM OF ART
P.O. Box 1838
Sarasota, Florida 33578

When John Ringling came to Sarasota in 1911, he was just one more millionaire building a winter home in sunny, booming Florida. He filled his thirty-three-room mansion with carved and gilded furniture, his own barber chair and a silver telephone. His bathtub was carved out of a single block of Italian marble, and finished off with gold faucets.

But when he died in 1936, the circus king bequeathed to the state a museum of priceless Baroque art. He also left the state his luxurious mansion, his property on Sarasota Bay and his fortune.

Ringling had been born seventy years earlier in Iowa, the youngest of seven sons of a German immigrant harness maker. At eighteen he and his brothers formed a small tent show. They did everything themselves, from pitching the tent to performing in the ring. The troupe was a success and in a few years the brothers expanded, eventually buying up most of the circuses in the country.

One year John Ringling decided to move the circus winter quarters and training center to Sarasota. When he announced that he

Ringling mansion

would build an art museum on his estate, everyone laughed. Ringling knew a great deal about performing clowns and elephants, but what did he know about art?

With the same determination that had turned a small troupe into the Greatest Show on Earth, he began to learn about this new interest. Within four years he bought 500 paintings and planned the building in which to display them.

Before construction could begin, the swampy site had to be cleared of water moccasins and alligators, and the land drained. At one point even the circus hands were called on for help.

Ringling said he hoped to create a place "like one of the old museums in Europe." He copied the style of an Italian villa. He visited villas in Venice, Genoa and Naples, where he bought old doorways, columns and marble for his architect to use.

The building is rectangular, surrounding a garden courtyard. On three sides there are display galleries; the fourth side is a covered walkway opening onto the garden and the sculptures in it.

It is logical that Ringling, a master showman, should fall in love with theatrical Baroque paintings. It is just as logical that the state of Florida should choose as museum director A. Everett Austin,

110

who had built a Baroque collection at the Wadsworth Atheneum. His new job was to turn a millionaire's hobby into an active, community-serving museum.

Austin set to work opening Ringling's home to the public, scheduling museum lectures and movies, and adding new works to the collection.

Ringling had bought many paintings by Peter Paul Rubens, but because he liked dramatic and heroic scenes, there were no portraits. And so Austin's first purchase was a Rubens portrait of the Archduke Ferdinand. The Spanish Ferdinand, who had become governor of the Netherlands just before he sat for this painting, was a military hero. He wears a suit of armor, but his sword is sheathed and he has laid his helmet aside and wears a civilian's hat. The military man is now the ruler. Typical Baroque elements in this painting are the heavy draperies in the background, the light gleaming on the archduke's armor and the sense of swirling movement that leads the eye from his face down along his sash and up again along his arms.

Among the Rubens paintings that Ringling had bought are Biblical scenes commissioned by the Infanta Isabella Clara Eugenia, sister of the King of Spain. (The archduke was Isabella's nephew, and she had preceded him as governor of the Netherlands.) The infanta asked Rubens to design eleven tapestries for a convent in Madrid. Exact copies of designs Rubens painted were woven of silk and wool in Brussels. Such designs—even when they are finished paintings—are called cartoons. The tapestries are still at the convent. Five of the cartoons were lost in a fire in 1731, two are in Paris at the Louvre and four are in Sarasota.

When Austin learned that a complete eighteenth-century theater from the town of Asolo, near Venice, was for sale, he decided he had to have it. The museum needed an auditorium. But more important, the little theater—at one time part of a palace—was delightfully elegant, a perfect companion to the museum's Ba-

111

Miniature Big Top

roque collection. And so the painted walls, decorated ceiling and other ornaments were taken down, crated and shipped to Sarasota. There the Asolo Theater was reconstructed inside a building especially made for it, next to the art museum. A lobby was added and furnished with chairs, tables, clocks and candelabra from the time of the original theater.

A new building has just been added to the Museum of Art. Although the style is Italian like the older buildings, there is now room for expansion to include contemporary art.

Appropriately, Mr. Ringling's estate also pays tribute to the circus. In addition to the art museum, there is the Museum of the Circus, which recalls circus history from its beginnings in ancient Greek and Roman festivals. Posters and handbills show the entertainers and animal trainers who performed at fairs and marketplaces in Europe centuries ago. Equipment as well as posters revive the excitement of American circuses, from the 1793 Philadelphia booking of Rickett's Circus seen by George Washington, through the many traveling shows of the nineteenth century. Several years ago the curator of this collection, who had been a Ringling clown,

112

suggested adding a circus "backyard." This is the behind-the-scenes area. Now you can see a cook house and a dining tent, a doctor's quarters, a harness maker's, a blacksmith's and a wheelwright's shop and dressing tents complete with spangled costumes. There are even the big elaborately decorated wagons that led the grand parades.

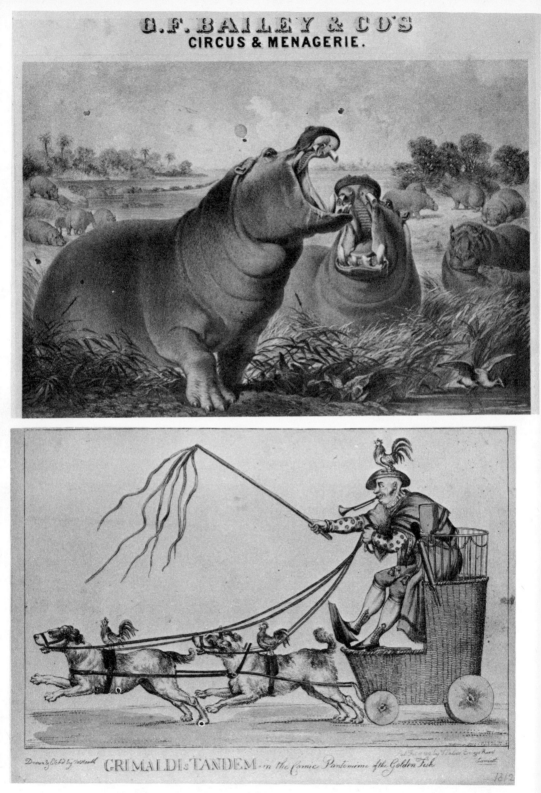

Early circus posters

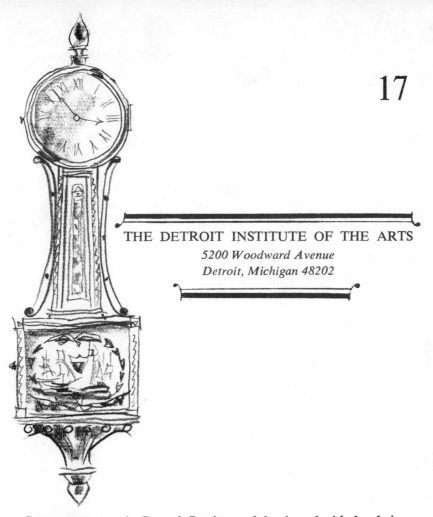

17

THE DETROIT INSTITUTE OF THE ARTS

5200 Woodward Avenue
Detroit, Michigan 48202

Some years ago the Detroit Institute of the Arts decided to bring the city's automobile industry right into the middle of the museum. Diego Rivera, a Mexican artist famous for his murals, was hired for the job and given the walls of the garden court as his canvas.

Rivera spent months visiting factories. He examined the machinery, watched men on the assembly lines, talked to workers and produced "The Making of a Motor." He painted rows and rows of machines. He painted a pattern of men and caught the rhythm of their actions, showing us what a busy and noisy factory is like.

One can read in these murals a city's pride in its industry and

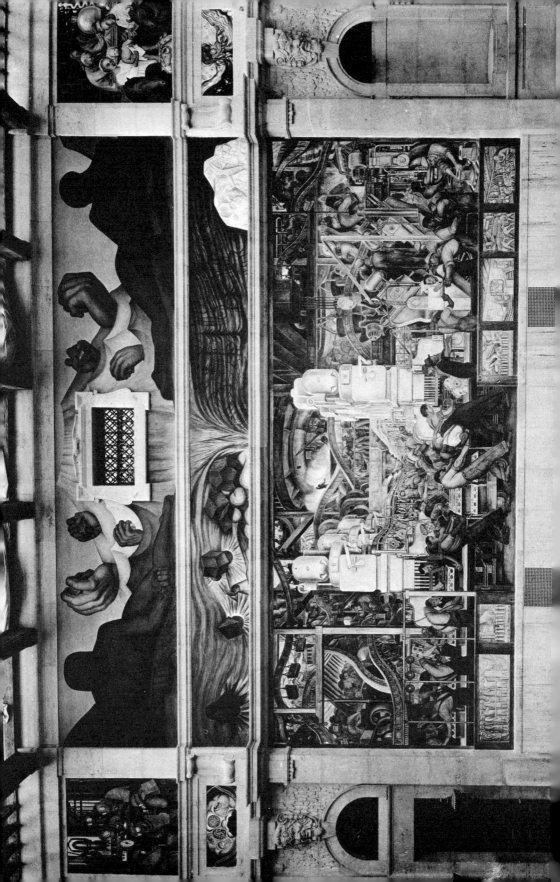

power. One can also read an artist's protest. The men Rivera painted seem to be part of the machinery. The machines tower over them. Gleaming metal seems more important than human beings. The artist is protesting against man's loss of individuality in a mass-production world.

The year was 1932 and the nation was suffering through the Depression. Factories were cutting back and many men were out of work. Those who could get jobs were glad to take them, at any price.

One of the factory workers Rivera had met had worn a funny hat, with a headband that read, "We want beer!" Rivera painted the man and his hat, but he turned the man's head slightly. The only words that can now be seen on the hatband are "We want," meaning "We are in need."

Everything on display at the Institute is a part of the story of man and art. The story goes back to prehistory and man's first recognition that his tools could look pleasing. The cave dweller who rubbed charcoal and bits of colored earth to outline familiar animals on his cave walls; the stoneworker who chipped his scrapers and his axheads in a pattern—these were the first artists. For fifty or sixty centuries, men have been making things beautiful and useful. In Detroit you will find furniture and fabrics, masks and puppets, jewelry and pottery, carpets and chandeliers, whole rooms or part of a wall, as well as paintings and sculptures.

At any one time, man has created in many different art forms. One of the best ways to learn about a civilization is to study the art it produced. Let's take sixteenth-century Europe.

Northern Europe was changing at the beginning of the sixteenth century. The Middle Ages were ending. A long succession of wars between local rulers was coming to an end. The nations we know today were beginning to take shape. Religion was the most important influence on people's lives, and wars were waged in the name of God as much as in the name of kings.

117

Diego Rivera mural

One can find built into a Detroit Institute gallery a small chapel from a French château built around 1500. A simple arch of carved stone forms the entrance. The coldness of the high stone walls is broken by stained-glass windows. The colors glow and give a sense of warmth and intimacy. A simple carved table holds a graceful statue of the Madonna and Child. There is quiet and peace and hope. The chapel was clearly a refuge where one could escape from daily problems and commune with God.

A glance at the armor collection will show you what kind of daily problems one might have wanted to escape from 500 years ago. The elaborate shiny steel suits are displayed on man-size figures. You can almost hear the clanking of elbow guards against arm-plates as the protected warriors stiffly mount their horses or march into battle.

While noblemen built châteaus with private chapels, and hired soldiers fought for them, peasants worked hard to farm the land. When they had a holiday or some other excuse for a celebration, they went at it with gusto and enjoyed themselves thoroughly. A peasant celebration is shown in "The Wedding Dance," Detroit's most famous painting. The artist was Pieter Breughel the Elder, of Flanders, the country now known as Belgium. His canvas is full of rhythm and movement. The tossing red and blue skirts of the white-aproned women, the saucy angles of their heads and caps and the swinging arms and legs of their sturdy partners create a lively scene.

During the early years of our own country, American life was patterned on the English. Colonists were carving a new nation out of wilderness, but those who could afford to furnished their homes with things brought across the Atlantic. American craftsmen became skilled at copying the styles of famous English cabinet-makers. A prosperous Colonial family once lived in Whitby Hall, a home that has been reconstructed and completely furnished within the museum.

118

Some of the pieces here are ingeniously designed to save space or perform two jobs at once. One table has a tilt top that raises to a vertical position and takes up very little space against a wall. At teatime, when it was needed for serving guests, it could be moved to the center of the room and opened up to hold plates and tea-cups. A small desk has a lift lid that conceals space for books, papers and writing materials.

From the same period is John Singleton Copley's painting of "Brook Watson and the Shark." Copley is best known for his portraits of Colonial New Englanders, but he left America to live in London which offered a greater intellectual life than any city here. There he met an Englishman, Brook Watson, who told him a spine-tingling tale. At the age of fourteen Watson was an apprentice seaman. His ship had docked in Havana. While he was swimming in the harbor he was attacked by a shark. One leg was bitten off below the knee before a group of men in a small boat could drive off the shark and rescue him. Watson's description was a vivid one, and Copley produced a dramatic scene.

Copley's first "Watson and the Shark" was an oil sketch that now belongs to the Metropolitan Museum of Art. Another copy hangs in the Boston Museum of Fine Arts. The copy that belonged to Watson himself went to Christ Hospital in London, and the one in Detroit is a somewhat smaller fourth copy. Copley also did a separate painting of the head of the standing Negro, and it too is in a gallery near the group picture.

In another gallery is a portrait of James Peale, by his brother Charles Willson Peale. James was also an artist. His specialty was miniatures—portraits small enough to stand on a table or fit into a traveling case. In the painting James is shown sitting at a table, studying a miniature he has just completed. An oil lamp lights his face and highlights the thin brush and a magnifying glass he used, on the table at his elbow.

The Detroit collection of American art is one of the most com-

119

"Watson and the Shark"

plete anywhere. It goes back even before the Colonial period, to the work of the Indians who lived here before Columbus, and shows work of every period since then. The institute is also collecting books, letters, diaries and other documents by and about our artists. The Archives of American Art will be a sort of superlibrary in which students and other museums can discover what any artist or his contemporaries had to say about his life, times and work.

120

Part III
SCIENCE

18

CRANBROOK INSTITUTE OF SCIENCE
Bloomfield Hills, Michigan 48013

As you approach the low sprawling building of the Cranbrook Institute of Science, you can't miss the large white rocks lining the semicircular path that leads around a garden, green with shrubbery. This is the Boulder Trail, and it is an introduction to a geology lesson that continues inside. Geology is just one of the many worlds of science that Cranbrook explores. The sun and stars, earth and air, water and rock, light and heat, plants, animals, and how people live are also subjects of exhibits.

The rocks along the Boulder Trail were left in this part of Michigan by glaciers. Glaciers are great moving masses of ice. During the Ice Age, a period that began 1,000,000 years ago, glaciers covered much of Europe, Asia and North America. Then, as the climate became warmer, they melted and moved north again. During the 75,000 years or so that the Ice Age lasted, glaciers moved southward and then retreated north several times. Today only the land near the poles is covered by glaciers. But they were among the most astounding forces to affect the earth since the beginning of time.

As each glacier retreated toward the polar regions, it left behind it the heaviest of the rocks it had been pushing. Smaller rocks and pebbles also being carried along in the mile-thick ice scratched deep lines into these boulders. At this museum you can stand in front of a 5¼-ton section of rock and feel the grooves in it— grooves that are several inches deep. Then you will have a good idea of the grinding action that was produced by the glacial ice. This enormous specimen was brought to Cranbrook from Kelley's Island in nearby Lake Erie. The surface of this rock is smooth. Sand and clay carried along in the glacier polished it. Their abrasive action on the hard rock can be compared to the effect of sandpaper and wax on wood.

Even after the glacier was gone, large "puddles" of ice still remained in land that had been "scooped out" by the glacier. As this ice melted, lakes were formed. Among the best-known glacial lakes are the five Great Lakes shared by the United States and Canada. Four of them—Superior, Huron, Michigan and Erie— touch on or extend into Michigan. The Ice Age and its results, therefore, have great meaning for most visitors to the Cranbrook museum.

In the galleries devoted to the earth's structure and history there is a model of the earth showing the four layers below the surface we live on. Around it smaller models show earlier ideas about the inside of the earth. These early theories were very dramatic. The earth's center was supposed to be filled with fire, surrounded by underground seas and rivers that fed water to the surface as whirlpools.

Today it is believed that the earth's center is a core made of a combination of iron and nickel. The temperature there is somewhere between 1,000 and 3,000 degrees Centigrade. Because of this extreme heat, the metals are in a molten or liquid state. The rim of this hot liquid core, which extends outward from the center for more than half the earth's total diameter, is about 1,800 miles

124

Exhibit shows structure of the earth.

below the earth's surface. It is surrounded by three thinner zones, the last of which is the crust on which we live.

Geology is the science concerned with the structure and history of the earth. It is also concerned with the minerals and rocks that make up the solid material of our earth. (Of the earth's surface, 30 percent is land; the other 70 percent is ocean.) Cranbrook's collection of rocks and minerals is one of the finest anywhere.

To understand what minerals and rocks are, it is first necessary to know a few scientific terms. An element is a basic substance which can combine with other elements, but which cannot be broken down into any simpler substance. Iron and mercury are two familiar elements.

Combinations of two or more elements are called compounds when those elements are in a fixed proportion to one another.

125

Water and salt are two familiar compounds. Water is always made up of two parts of hydrogen to one part of oxygen; salt is always made up of one part of sodium to one part of chlorine.

Minerals are the forms in which elements or compounds occur naturally. Those minerals that consist of only one element are known as native elements. Gold, silver and sulfur are examples. Graphite and diamond are two different forms of the element carbon. These native elements, and others, can be seen in a special display at Cranbrook.

But most minerals are compounds. Topaz, for example, has the chemical name of aluminum silicate, because it is a combination of the elements aluminum and silica. One of the rarest individual specimens in the Cranbrook collection is a 100-pound white topaz crystal that came from Brazil. Most topaz is yellow, owing to other chemical compounds that are mixed in with the minerals; the Cranbrook topaz is unusual for its color as well as its size.

A rock may be a single mineral or combination of two or more minerals. The display of rocks illustrates the most common varieties, and explains how the action of heat, water, other rocks and pressure may cause certain types of rock to change into others. Under heat and pressure, limestone becomes marble. Both are rock forms of the compound calcium carbonate. Chalk is still another form of this compound.

A very dramatic exhibit uses light to show some hidden qualities of rocks and minerals. Thin slices of various minerals have been mounted in a transparent display case. A light is beamed from behind. The mineral pieces are so thin that light comes through them the way light comes through a photographic slide in a projector. You can easily see the fascinating structure that is usually hidden. In a cross section of tourmaline, a mineral used in jewelry, triangles of contrasting color show the pattern by which the stone grew. Cross sections of mica show bits of several minerals that became embedded in it.

126

100-pound Brazilian topaz

If you walk through the main gallery floor, you will come to Physics Hall. Look for a large curved mirror that distorts your reflection, and a sign marking the entrance: THE BEHAVIOR OF MATTER: THE FIELD OF PHYSICS.

When this hall was being planned, it was decided that the physics exhibits would show things actually happening. Demonstrations would be going on right in the gallery. Visitors would be allowed to work many of these. But since delicate equipment is needed for some, at least one demonstrator would always be in Physics Hall to help out and answer questions.

One of the most striking of these demonstrations is the Foucault pendulum. This is a replica of the apparatus used by a Frenchman,

127

Jean Foucault, in 1851 to prove that the earth rotates. He suspended a 200-foot pendulum so that its weighted bottom, moving freely back and forth, would mark its path in sand spread on the floor beneath it. But instead of tracing the same path in the sand on every swing, it kept marking off new lines always somewhat to the clockwise side of its previous path. At the museum the demonstrator sets the Foucault pendulum and notes the time. While you look at some of the other exhibits, the pendulum continues to swing. If you look at it a few minutes later, you will see that the pendulum's swing is no longer where it was when it was put in motion. While the pendulum, suspended from a point in the ceiling above, has continued to swing in the same plane, the earth and everything on it has been moving.

A room off the physics gallery is known as the Atomarium. It is a unique science theater where the smallest known particles of matter are put "onstage," as it were, to perform for you. The Atomarium is the first of its kind in America, but it is based on similar science theaters in Stockholm and Vienna. It does for the microcosmos—the infinitely small world of matter—what a planetarium does for the macrocosmos or universe.

An atom is the smallest part into which a substance can be divided and still behave as that substance. The word is Greek for "indivisible." The atoms in any element are all alike. Compounds are made up of atoms of different elements. The smallest part of a compound substance that still behaves like that substance is called a molecule. A molecule is the basic combination of the atoms of the two or more elements in a compound.

In the Atomarium you will hear about the early philosophers and scientists and their ideas regarding the structure of the unseen atom—a tiny bit of matter so small that it could only be imagined, but not seen until very, very powerful microscopes were developed. You can look through such a microscope here, and actually see atoms.

128

The demonstrator shows you colored beads to illustrate the basic building blocks that atoms are made of. These building blocks are called proton, neutron and electron. The number of electrons an atom has determines the behavior of that atom. Electrons can be borrowed, shared or exchanged between atoms, binding them together to form groups of atoms, or molecules. Chemistry is the science that explores the behavior of the electrons of atoms.

The lecturer shines a special flashlight on a specially treated screen, to draw diagrams showing you how the protons, neutrons and electrons of several different atoms are arranged. He also demonstrates some of the equipment used to confirm the theories of atom behavior that scientists accept today.

On the wall is a big chart showing all the elements, from hydrogen, which is number 1, to lawrencium, number 103. The chemical symbol for each element comes from the first one or two letters of its Latin name—hydrogen is simply H, while gold is Au, for *aurum*. The same chart appears over the demonstration table in Physics Hall.

Among the demonstrations in the physics gallery that you can perform yourself is one that uses Ping-Pong balls in a tall glass tube. When you send a jet of air up into the tube, the Ping-Pong balls start jumping around and bumping into one another. This is a model of what happens when a substance is heated. The molecules absorb the heat energy and translate it into motion, known as kinetic energy. This is what happens when water is heated in a pot. Long before the boiling point is reached, the water molecules start rushing around and bumping into one another. You can notice the movement of the water even before it begins to boil.

The display with the headline ELECTROMAGNETIC WAVES shows you some surprising things about light and color.

You will learn that light moves in waves, very much like the waves of moving water formed when a pebble is dropped into a pond. Light waves (or rays) are of different lengths and the length

129

determines the color we see. The longest waves we are able to see register on our eyes as red, and the shortest as violet. In between are the other colors of the visible spectrum—orange, yellow, green, blue and all the shades in between. We see an object as yellow because it reflects the yellow wavelength of the light shining on it from a source such as the sun or an electric light. The yellow object absorbs all light waves of other lengths. An object that appears to us as black is absorbing all the light that shines on it, and reflecting none. A white object reflects all light hitting it, and absorbs none.

But there are also waves that are longer and waves that are shorter than those in the visible spectrum. Beyond the red rays are the infrared, which are too long to register as color in the human eye, but which we can feel as heat waves. Even longer are radio waves. At the other extreme are ultraviolet, X and gamma rays, too short to be seen.

Now go back to Mineral Hall, and enter the room to the right of the transparency case. The room is dark, but you will notice spots of beautifully glowing colors. Ultraviolet light, which you cannot see, is shining on a special group of minerals. Most familiar substances cannot be seen in ultraviolet light, because there are no visible light wavelengths to be reflected back to us. But some rare substances absorb the very short waves of invisible ultraviolet light, and then change them so they can be reflected back as longer rays of visible light. The new light waves come back to us in colors—colors that are eerily bright, different from the colors we ordinarily see. Ordinary colors are only reflected, while these colors are actually light waves made within the minerals themselves, out of the ultraviolet light they received. Substances that react to light this way are called fluorescent.

Now go into the room on the other side of the transparency case. The light in the room is automatically controlled to alternate periods of darkness with periods of ordinary light, of ultraviolet light and a combination of the two. You will notice that several of the

130

large stones here continue to glow after all light is turned off. They have absorbed the light waves and are reflecting them back. It is almost as though the light waves have been stored up. This phenomenon is known as phosphorescence.

The phosphorescence exhibit, like everything else here, is an expression of the "new vision of museum usefulness" that guided the Cranbrook's founding and has guided it ever since.

19

THE ADLER PLANETARIUM AND
ASTRONOMICAL MUSEUM
900 East Achsah Bond Drive
Chicago, Illinois 60605

MOREHEAD PLANETARIUM
University of North Carolina
Chapel Hill, North Carolina 27514

SPACE TRANSIT PLANETARIUM
Museum of Science and Natural History
3280 South Miami Avenue
Miami, Florida 33129

There is something about the spectacle of the night sky above
that has always aroused man's curiosity and sense of wonder. By
the early part of the twentieth century, scientists had unlocked
many of the secrets of the universe. Then they sought a dramatic
way to show the public some of the things they had learned. They
developed a complicated instrument called a planetarium. It
could project pictures of the stars, moon and planets onto the
white underside of an enormous sphere.

In addition to the projector, there were seats for the public inside the sphere. It was a sort of theater and was also called a planetarium. Here the drama of the skies could be acted out, at the same time as the scientific story of the universe was told.

Chicago was the first city in the United States to have a planetarium.

Long before the planetarium instrument was invented, men were making models of the planets in motion. Models of one sort or another date back to a time shortly after 1543, when Copernicus demonstrated that all the planets, including the earth, move around the sun. Copernicus, for this reason, is considered the father of modern astronomy. His discoveries led to the construction of moving models of the solar system. These models consisted of globes of various sizes joined together with gears. Eventually one such construction was made in England for the fourth Earl of Orrery. It was referred to as an orrery and the term has stuck. A great number and variety of orreries are in use today, at planetariums and in schools.

Throughout the eighteenth and nineteenth centuries, orreries were produced in Europe and in the United States. David Rittenhouse of Philadelphia made several that were particularly fine. One of them, built in 1769, showed the relative positions of the planets with great accuracy. It also demonstrated the movements of the moon and computed the year, month and day of past and future eclipses. This mechanism is now at the University of Pennsylvania.

But the orrery showed only an outside view of the solar system. What scientists now wanted was a means of providing an inside view, so that one could actually feel he was part of the universe. Devices called celestial globes were built to provide this inside view. One variety consisted of a sphere pricked with pinholes to represent stars. The viewer looked in through a special opening and saw a pinpoint of light on the opposite interior wall. The most famous of these was built in 1699 by Erhardt Weigel, a professor

133

of astronomy at the University of Jena in Germany. It was eventually brought to Philadelphia, to the Franklin Institute.

There was another kind of celestial globe big enough for an observer to enter. Weigel built one of these also. It could produce the effect of meteors, rain, hail, thunder, lightning and even volcanoes.

About sixty years later, an American built an enormous hollow sphere that rotated when it was turned by hand from the outside. Constellations were painted on its inside walls, and perforations represented stars. Light from outside the globe showed through these perforations and could be seen by viewers inside. The spectators stood on a stationary platform at the center of the astronomical machine, which was moved around and about them. A motor-driven globe that did the same thing was popular at the Chicago Academy of Sciences early in the twentieth century.

The idea of using a stationary dome and then arranging many small projectors to throw images of stars onto that dome originated in Germany. The optical firm of Carl Zeiss in Jena invented an unbelievably complicated instrument that could reveal to the naked eye not only the stars, but the sun, the moon and the planets, all in their proper places for any moment of any year of any century. The first model, which could show the skies—past, present and future—for only *one* place on earth, began to perform in 1924. If you were in Jena, Germany, you could see the stars of any year, but only as they looked over Jena.

Soon the machine would be adjusted to project the stars and planets in the right position for any place on earth. Soon it would be possible to sit, for example, in Los Angeles, and view the heavens as they actually looked to Columbus in Spain on the eve of his departure for the New World.

Max Adler, a prosperous Chicago businessman, was among the many Americans who flocked to Germany when they heard of the new astronomy machine from Jena. Because he was concerned

134

Antique quadrant, astrolabe, celestial sphere and sundial

about what he called the "meager knowledge" of the public about the planets and the stars, and because he believed that "under the heavens everything is interrelated, even as each of us to the other," he determined to give the people of Chicago a museum of astronomy in which the principal exhibit would be the new Zeiss planetarium instrument.

Inside the Adler Planetarium and Astronomical Museum an audience of 500 people can see the stars and planets perform.

The story of how modern navigational and astronomical instruments have developed from much simpler devices is told in an extensive group of exhibits. The Adler Astronomical Museum has the world's finest collection of historic and antique equipment of this kind. Scientists and sailors of ages past used sundials, calendars, quadrants, telescopes and compasses which can be seen here.

Astronauts Lovell and Borman study stars at Morehead Planetarium.

It is a far cry from the simple instruments used by Columbus to the complex control board of a modern space vehicle. But the stars in the heavens help guide our navigators in outer space just as they guided our navigators on the vast seas. Several years ago officials of the National Aeronautics and Space Administration (NASA) realized this, and began working with one of our planetariums on a program to teach the astronauts star identification for navigational purposes.

In 1960 the first seven astronauts of Project Mercury began their study of astronomy at the Morehead Planetarium, on the University of North Carolina campus. The training program was later commented on by astronauts who completed voyages in space. Major Edward H. White II, who was the first American to walk in space during the Gemini 4 flight, suggested that the stars as shown at the Morehead be brightened. "Bring them up a bit more," he told the planetarium's director, who was operating the controls of the Zeiss projector. "Up there they're so bright it's amazing."

A spaceman on his way to the moon sees the earth as one of the heavenly bodies. To show the earth as it would look to a viewer from any point in the solar system, intricate new devices had to be attached to the Morehead's old projector. Sitting in a simulated space capsule in the planetarium chamber, astronauts get a chance to test their ability to navigate with the guidance of the earth, moon and stars.

A new type of instrument that can show how the earth looks from space as the Morehead's changed projector can has now been produced, and one of these is in the Space Transit Planetarium in Miami, Florida. When you enter the star theater here, you may be about to take a trip from one planet to another, or from the earth to the moon. A moon trip in Miami starts with a simulated blast-off from Cape Kennedy. Then the entire planetarium chamber in which you are sitting seems to go into orbit around the earth. The stars tilt back, forth and sideways as the make-believe spaceship you are in seems to roll, pitch and yaw. Eventually you continue your journey, go into orbit around the moon and finally land on it. There is a very bright planet in the sky that you have never seen before. It is Earth.

20

DENVER MUSEUM
OF NATURAL HISTORY
City Park
Denver, Colorado 80206

The drama of man's cruel disregard of nature and the struggle to correct his mistakes are vividly captured in an exhibit at the Denver Museum of Natural History. To understand the way in which this one exhibit sums up the important part natural science museums have played in wildlife conservation, you should know a story that begins around 1890 on an island in the Pacific 850 miles northwest of Honolulu.

The island, called Laysan, was once famous among ornithologists—scientists whose special field of study is bird life—for its remarkable nesting colonies of sea- and shorebirds. It is believed that there were about a million of them: petrels, shearwaters, grayback terns and white fairy terns, red-footed boobies, great frigate birds, also known as man-o'-war birds, and, most famous of all, the white Laysan albatrosses and the dark black-footed albatrosses. These seabirds made long flights over the ocean—perhaps thousands of miles—during their seasonal migrations. They came to Laysan to perform their mating rituals, build their nests, lay eggs and hatch their young. There were also plovers, bristle-thighed curlews, gulls and red phalaropes. These are shorebirds whose island-to-island flights brought them to the sands of Laysan to nest.

In addition there were five species—a teal, a rail, a miller bird, a honey eater and a finch—that could be found nowhere else in the world. The teal (a kind of duck) and the rail were unable to fly. The others could manage only short distances in the air. These five had lived on Laysan, isolated from related species, for such a long period of time that they had developed in ways that made them unique. They were completely different in many ways from even their closest relatives.

Before 1890 few people came to the island. It was peaceful and undisturbed. Then the Hawaiian government agreed to lease Laysan to a guano company for twenty years.

Guano consists mostly of bird droppings, mixed with some feathers and bones. It is used for fertilizer. The business of collecting guano and selling it was a very profitable one. The man in charge of the guano operation was a German captain named Schlemmer. When the sailors who came in ships to collect the guano left, and put in at different ports, they talked about the great number of birds they had seen. Soon news of the birds reached the ears of feather hunters, who knew how much money could be made selling feathers to decorate ladies' hats.

It was not long before the island became a place of slaughter for hundreds of thousands of birds. The feather hunters were mostly Japanese. One of their weapons was a simple club with which they would beat down the albatrosses while the birds sat on their nests. They cut off the wings of those beautiful dark-eyed creatures and either left them in their nests to bleed alongside their eggs, or threw them, crippled but still alive, into a large cistern where they died slowly and in great pain.

But nature is strong beyond belief. Despite the slaughter, the five rare species continued somehow to survive, although reduced in number. So did most of the migratory birds. The enemy that finally succeeded in destroying them was man's heedlessness of nature's laws.

To supply additional food for the sailors who came to Laysan, the manager of the guano company, Captain Schlemmer, brought rabbits to the island. What he was doing, without knowing it, was upsetting the island's ecological balance. Ecology is the study of the relationships of living things to the world of which they are a part—their relationships to plants and animals and also to air, water, mountains, soil—everything living and nonliving which makes up their environment. Before the rabbits came, Laysan Island was ecologically balanced, which means there was an adjustment among its living beings and their surroundings that is similar to the adjustment in a balanced aquarium. The living things were in harmony with each other and the island, ensuring the survival of each species.

But the rabbits did not belong there. They had been brought by man, not nature. Having no natural enemies there, the rabbits quickly multiplied and soon overran the island. They consumed the vegetation so rapidly and completely that it was not replaced by natural growth.

The plants had kept the sand from shifting about. Several varieties of the island's birds nested in sand burrows. Now a high wind could fill the entrances with loose sand, smothering the birds inside.

By 1912 there was in the United States the beginning of an understanding of the need for an active conservation program. Many species of animals had become extinct or were on the verge of extinction because of man's thoughtlessness. People began to realize that those creatures whose lives were threatened must be protected and saved.

When the story of Laysan became known, the Biological Survey of the United States Department of Agriculture sent an expedition to the island. Its mission was twofold: to identify and count the bird population, and to kill off the rabbits. Signed on as cook for this expedition was a college sophomore, Alfred E. Bailey, who would one day become the director of Denver's museum. He collected specimens of Laysan's rare birds and brought them home.

Unfortunately, the expedition did not exterminate all the rabbits. Some escaped and multiplied. During the next ten years the island was turned into a wasteland. Birds died of starvation and disease, and so did the rabbits. But over a period of time, Laysan's vegetation began to reappear. Species of migrating birds came again to the island. But of the five rare native species, three—the Laysan curved-bill honey eater, the flightless rail, and the little miller bird—were gone forever.

The collection of bird specimens brought home by young Alfred Bailey was given to the Denver Museum. At the Laysan Island

Diorama shows royal albatross at Campbell Island.

exhibit, the birds look lifelike and beautiful. They are a reminder that many species throughout the world are threatened with extinction.

The Laysan exhibit is, of course, just one feature of this fine middle-size museum. Entomology—the study of insect life—and botany—the study of plants—are two subjects particularly well covered. Mammals and birds have been of special interest at the Denver Museum ever since it was organized back in 1897. The animals of North and South America and the Arctic—bison, deer, bears, peccaries and mountain lions—all are to be found here. Not surprisingly, Colorado's animals, rocks, minerals and vegetation are also given considerable attention. A favorite display is in Walter C. Mead Hall. Here one can trace the changes in animal and plant life from the high mountain tops down to the desert.

Just as the clue to the tragedy of Laysan Island was ecological balance, the clue to many of Denver's animal displays is ecological grouping. The displays show the animal not as star performer but as a sort of featured player in a drama involving many of the plants and animals of the same region. There may be as many as 10,000 parts to one display, each made separately and painstakingly of paper, wood, wax or newer plastic materials. Birds, insects, reptiles, fish, mice, leaves, flowers and a long, long list are vividly and exactly lifelike. Art and science work together to produce such an exhibit. The people who perform the magic of creating these displays are called preparators.

Another important activity that goes on behind the scenes in a natural history museum is fieldwork. The Biological Survey that went to Laysan Island was a field trip. An archeological expedition is another kind of field trip. The curator of archeology at the Denver Museum was recently in charge of a dig in an area where tools and bison bones were found. Study of the find showed that a group of Indians hunted and butchered game here, perhaps as early as 8000 B.C. Their prey was a species of bison now extinct.

142

The gallery devoted to archeology is concerned with prehistoric people of the Americas. A monument made by people of the great Mayan civilization about 1,300 years ago came from British Honduras. It is a great limestone slab, known as a stele, elaborately carved with designs that are now faint and worn down by age. Careful study of these and similar carvings has shown that the Mayans developed a method of picture writing, an accurate calendar and a system of mathematics, based on the number 20, far in advance of anything then known in Western Europe.

This gallery also displays one of the most famous archeological finds of North America. It is a block of stone in which the rib bones of an extinct bison were found—along with a piece of a flint weapon. Because it was known that the ribs were from a species of bison that died out about 10,000 years ago, the presence of the weapon proved that there were men in the New World then. Dug up in 1926 near Folsom, New Mexico, this was the first definite proof that men were living here that long ago. Until this find was made, it was quite generally believed that human life on this continent went back only about 3,000 years. Archeological finds made in the forty years since Folsom man was discovered, and better methods of dating long-buried bones and artifacts, lead today's scientists to believe that men were here 30,000 or perhaps even 40,000 years ago.

Mastodons roamed about in those days, and dinosaurs thousands of years earlier. You can see their skeletons and those of other strange creatures in exhibits showing the succession of life through the ages. They are another reason why Denver's Museum of Natural History, although not one of the biggest, is one of the best of its kind in the country.

21

ARIZONA-SONORA DESERT MUSEUM
Tucson Mountain Park (P.O. Box 5602)
Tucson, Arizona 85703

Many people are surprised to find that plants and animals flourish in the desert. They know that the single most important thing about a desert is the scarcity of water, and that water is necessary for life. But living things have developed many ways of surviving in an environment where only a very little moisture is available to them.

Fourteen miles west of the city of Tucson is the Arizona-Sonora Desert Museum. Just inside its entrance you will find the Orientation Room. Here you will discover seventeen ways in which plants and animals conserve water and are protected from the extreme heat of the desert day and the extreme cold of the night. A large relief map shows the extent of the Sonoran Desert, which is the subject of every exhibit in this museum. It stretches for 120,000 miles through northern Mexico and the southwestern part of the United States.

Along one wall are two displays which point up dramatically the similarity between desert creatures of America and those of Australia and Africa. In one of the displays, you see the thorny devil, an Australian lizard. Press a button and before your eyes, it becomes the very similar horned toad of Arizona. In the next show-case you watch as the horned viper (a reptile) and the jerboa (a rodent) of the Sahara Desert become, at the push of another button, the sidewinder and the kangaroo rat of the Sonora. (The special effects in these dissolving displays are created with a complicated arrangement of mirrors and lights.)

In the Amphibian Room and the Aquarium you can make the surprising discovery that even water-dwelling creatures live in the desert. Among them are the Colorado River toad, the desert pupfish, the tiger salamander and other aquatic or semiaquatic species. Many of them are shown in a new kind of display, called a living diorama, developed here at the Desert Museum. Real animals splash about behind heavy glass walls. A realistically painted background (done, of course, with waterproof colors) shows the natural setting of each. The rocks and plants in the foreground, where the animals live, are both real and man-made. Rivers, springs and rain puddles are created with water that is aerated and continually circulated by an elaborate pumping device.

In the Small Animal Room you will come upon a giant hair scorpion and learn that the sting of this frightening creature is, although painful, usually harmless. But take a good look at the smaller, colorless scorpion. He is dangerous and should be avoided. You will see a tarantula, the largest species of spider in the world. It may surprise you to learn tarantulas are not dangerous—at least, not the ones found in the United States. And you will see the diamondback rattlesnake, whose bite *is* dangerous, and learn that it is nevertheless very valuable as an exterminator of

Coyotes are among 750 living animals at Arizona-Sonora.

rodents. To discover why the rattler got its name, experiment with the life-size rubber reptile coiled on the table in the center of the room. At the push of a button, its tail shakes and rattles, in a convincing imitation of the real snake about to strike.

On one wall you see a small glass-covered opening with what appears to be a gun stuck into it. Behind the glass all is dark, until you pull the trigger. The gun is really a spotlight, and by its light you can just make out a cluster of vampire bats hanging from the roof of a cave. They are the only mammals in the world who eat nothing but blood. These bats are real, and they get a real dish of their favorite food every day.

Outside are the large animal dens. As you walk past them, you can see the coyote, a beast so common that you may pass one not far from the museum. Others, such as the ocelot, jaguar and black bear, are more rarely seen.

You may watch the inhabitants of Prairie Dog Village and Chulo Town, two animal communities with large pens separated

146

from human visitors only by a low wall. Prairie dogs are engaging and amusing little creatures. These small rodents ranged far and wide through the Southwest until they were forced out by cattle ranches. The coatimundi, known in Mexico as the chulo, is related to the raccoon, which you can believe when you look at its snout. But if you look at its other end, the long tail may easily remind you of a monkey.

The path that leads past deer and antelope, and past the bird enclosures, brings you to a wooden doorway almost hidden beneath a mound of rocks. This is the entrance to the Desert Tunnel. Here you will find creatures seldom seen in the daytime. In the unfriendly environment of the desert many animals spend much of their time underground, in burrows and tunnels and caves, where they are protected from harsh extremes of temperature. Most come out only at night to forage for food.

As you go in and down a ramp, your eyes blink to adjust to the darkness. Dim lights near the floor help you find the handrail on your right. The rail is your guide to the exhibits in the dark tunnel. As you walk along and lean on it facing glass-covered openings in the wall, lights go on so that you can read labels and see the animals in their underground homes. Rattlesnakes go about their slithery business only inches from your face. A kit fox, surprised by the sudden light shining into his burrow, stares out at you with huge eyes. In the pack rat's burrow you can see the bits of wood and food he has taken from his neighbor, the porcupine, and stashed away.

Farther along, real bats hang by tiny sharp claws from the ceiling of a bat cave, complete with imitation stalactites and stalagmites (made by taking molds of real formations in a real cave, and casting the imitations of plaster). Unlike the vampires in the main building, these bats are fruit eaters. Melon and other food are left in a large wire cage above the cave where they sleep the day away. When night falls, these nocturnal creatures are ready

147

to leave their cave for the cage aboveground and out of doors. Here they feed and exercise until dawn.

Other inhabitants of the tunnel also have outdoor play yards where they may stretch during their active nighttime hours. But during the day the animals prefer the comfort and darkness of their man-made dens.

On the left side of the tunnel you may take a belowground look at desert plants. The plants themselves are outside, above the tunnel. But their roots have been set into cases of soil placed against a glass wall so that you can see root shapes and how they grow. The job of the roots is to locate precious water and circulate it to the growing plant. Naturally, roots require darkness. But a push button lights up each exhibit and its label for you. Standing in front of a root system, you may look through the periscope set into the glass wall to get an aboveground view of the plant.

From the tunnel a trail leads to the beginning of Water Street. Here you will find dramatic demonstrations of how the desert uses water, and how water can be both helpful and harmful. You enter a vine-covered shed where there are push buttons for you to press. The first sets off a tape recording explaining what you are about to see. Press the lower button if you have any questions; a museum teacher in the green tower off to the south will hear and answer you by a sort of walkie-talkie arrangement. He can see you through a telescope.

Throughout the Water Street exhibition you will find other buttons to push. At a rainfall demonstration, a button sets off a recording. You may hear that "the greatest original source of usable water is rainfall. Did you know that the average annual rainfall in Arizona provides eleven times as much water as the entire state uses in a year? Or did you know that a very high percentage of that rainfall was carried away to other parts of the world through evaporation and atmospheric action before it could be used by plants, wildlife or man?"

148

One exhibit shows how different kinds of rain gauges are used to measure rainfall. You are invited to use a gauge yourself. You look through a telescope at a gauge set up in the distance. When you press a black button, an electric circuit is completed, causing water to fall into the gauge. As it falls, a bucket attached to the gauge tips whenever two hundredths of an inch of water is added.

One of the most effective displays shows the power of water, and how it can be either good or bad for the land. Through each of three tall glass tubes, about 40 drops of water per minute fall from a height of eight feet. Below each tube is a small sample of soil. Forty drops per minute add up to 1½ gallons each day, 53 gallons a month.

Through the first tube the drops of water fall on a plot of very grassy soil. Blades of grass break up the relentlessly falling drops, and grass roots hold the earth in place. No soil erosion occurs, and a flashing green light and green-colored label tell you that this is a "safe" plot.

A yellow light signals "warning" above the second soil sample. Here the clumps of grass are too far apart for the roots to hold the soil down. A label tells you that the grass can be saved if more is planted.

The soil in the third plot is completely barren, with an irregularly shaped hole in the center. A red light signals "danger." There is no plant cover at all, and the unprotected earth has already been splashed away. A splashboard measures the distance the soil particles travel when hit by waterdrops. A label tells the sad story: "Bare, loose soil is commonly thrown to a height of 2 or 3 feet and to horizontal distances of 5 feet in normal rainfall. The total energy of raindrops, falling at a rate of one-tenth of an inch per hour, has been estimated at 100 horsepower per acre."

Almost at the end of Water Street you pass the control tower from which your questions have been answered. Then you come to a small darkened room where you will see color slides. The recorded narration tells you that when rain does come to the desert it comes in cloudbursts that create flash floods and rapidly running streams that carry off valuable topsoil and plants. However, where there is vegetation, roots hold onto the soil. It is up to man to provide the plants that will hold soil to the land.

To show what can be planted to rescue the desert and beautify it at the same time, the museum has a delightful garden. In the spring and early summer the yucca, prickly pear, ocatillo, cholla and other plants burst into bloom.

But even if you live in an arid region, don't try to plant the saguaro—the tall, branching cactus that you see everywhere about. Its waxy white flowers, so beautiful in the spring, are the state flower of Arizona. The saguaro is such a slow grower that you will have to wait years for it to grow an inch. The splendid specimens you see all about you, 40 or 50 feet high, are probably 150 years old.

A "garden" of desert plants

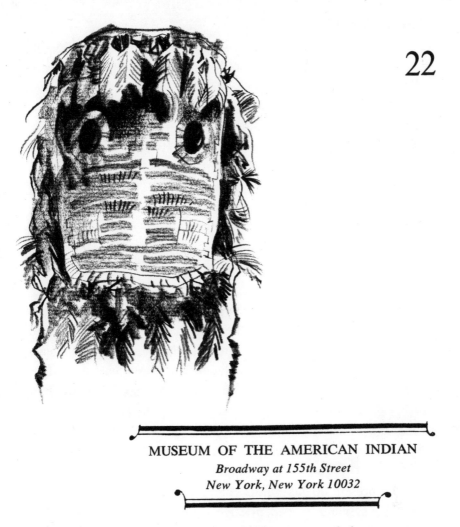

22

MUSEUM OF THE AMERICAN INDIAN
Broadway at 155th Street
New York, New York 10032

The Museum of the American Indian is one of six gray stone buildings surrounding a courtyard on a hillside in upper Manhattan. The first thing that distinguishes it from its neighbors is the colorful totem pole which stands in front of the building, just beyond the entrance.

This pole, painted blue, white, red, brown and black, once stood in front of the house of Chief Eagle of the Haida Tribe on Prince of Wales Island, off the coast of southern Alaska. It is 43 feet 5 inches tall, and weighs 4,490 pounds. But it was not created

151

to stand simply as an impressive decoration in front of the chief's house. It was, in fact, a very special kind of nameplate, identifying the owner of the house, listing his honors and mentioning several of his ancestors and the sacred stories of his clan.

The figure at the top of the pole is, not surprisingly, an eagle. Chief Eagle was believed to possess the bird's power. The bird protected him. It was his "sign" and spirit. It was his totem.

Reading down the pole, the carvings just below the eagle look like thick disks stacked one on top of another. These are called prestige cylinders, because they indicate the importance of the chief and some of his achievements. A chief was entitled to these status symbols after he was the host at a feast known as the potlatch. This was a feast that might last for several days or even weeks. A rival chief and his entire household were the guests. They were entertained and served great quantities of food. They were given many gifts—carved boxes, blankets, clothing, and servants. The more a chief was able to present to his guests, the greater became his prestige. Even his servants gained prestige by belonging to such an important chief. The guest chief, on the other hand, slipped down the social ladder and could regain his position only by giving a return potlatch that would be even more elaborate. The potlatch was a way of showing power as well as wealth. It is believed to have served as a substitute for war.

Chief Eagle's pole—with its prestige cylinders recording the potlatches he gave—was carved about 100 years ago. Most totem poles were produced between 1830 and 1900; not many were made earlier.

152

Next on Chief Eagle's totem pole are carvings of animal folk heroes: Grizzly and his wife, Frog Person and Beaver. All of them were totems of Chief Eagle's ancestors. At the very bottom of the pole is the figure of a hunter. And now that you have read the pole, it is time to go inside.

A long case to the left of the entrance contains an exhibit which tells the story of wampum. Everybody knows, or thinks he knows, what wampum is. "Indian money, of course," we say quickly if we are asked. But do you know that wampum is also a combination history book, newspaper and legal document? Wampum beads were made of pieces cut from the purple and white shell of the hard-shell clam, purple along the edge, white at the center. Then the shell pieces were ground into tiny cylinders. Holes were either cut through them with very small stone drills or bored with the end of a reed or slender sticks rotated with light downward pressure in sand sprinkled over the shell. The hole was bored from both ends of the bead to the middle. Then the beads were rubbed with fine sand and pieces of buckskin to polish them. Finally they were strung on cords made of vegetable fiber or animal sinew. The Algonquian word *wampumpeak*, from which the shortened "wampum" comes, actually means "white string of shell beads."

Several strings were woven into wampum belts. These belts were exchanged by tribes living on or near the Atlantic coast to confirm alliances, record treaties and provide formal records of important events. They were also given as expressions of sympathy at the death of a notable tribesman. Each tribe had a keeper of the wampum, whose duty it was to "read" the belts that belonged to the tribe, and remind the people of important events in their history.

Among the belts belonging to the Museum of the American Indian (which has the largest wampum collection anywhere) are two that were given to William Penn in 1683 at the Treaty of

153

Mask of False Face Society

Shakawaxon. This treaty set the boundaries of land purchased from the Lenapes by Penn and his Quakers. One belt has a meandering design that indicates the mountain and river boundaries of the treaty area. The design of crosses on the second belt is said to indicate the land itself. Eighteen separate strands, and more than 1,000 individual beads, make up this second belt. A third Penn treaty belt, showing two men holding hands to signify friendship between the Englishmen and the Indians, belongs to the Historical Society of Pennsylvania.

Near the wampum exhibit is a display of masks, colorful and grotesque, which belonged originally to the False Face Society of the Iroquois. The masks represent heroes of legends who have the power to cure disease and drive off evil spirits. The power of the masks was considered especially great because they were carved from living trees. It was reasoned, therefore, that they had the power of life. On one side of the display is a section of a tree trunk. It shows how the mask was carved right into the trunk after the bark was stripped off. Later the mask was cut away from the tree, painted and perhaps decorated with bits of metal or shell (set in as eyeballs) and human or horsetail hair.

The Iroquois believed that a person's soul leaves his body during sleep and wanders about, and that in a dream the dreamer is al-

154

lowed to watch the soul's journey through the spirit world. Because dreams were regarded as messages from the supernatural, it was important that instructions received in them be carried out promptly. A man might envision a mask in a dream, and set about carving it the next day.

During a healing ceremony the members wore their masks, sang, danced and attracted the attention of the spirits with rattles made from the shell of the snapping turtle. These rattles were not shaken, but were hit against the singer's bench to produce a sound.

Although the rituals of the False Face Society began in prehistoric times, they are still being practiced in upper New York State today. There is a mask in the museum's collection made as recently as 1950. The types of masks have not changed over the years.

The branch of science most concerned with the traditional Indian way of life is anthropology. Anthropologists have lived with tribespeople, interviewed them and observed their customs. They have studied family and tribal history, as well as legends, songs, prayers, rituals and ceremonies. Anthropologists call the way of life of a people its culture. This term includes such things as how the people get their food and how they prepare, serve and eat it. It includes the stories of how their group began. It includes the kinds of houses they live in, the clothes they wear, games they play, songs they sing, weapons they use, gods they worship—and just about everything else you can think of. Each of these is known as a culture trait. Today many anthropologists are trying to help the Indians—there are about 600,000 in the country—hold onto some of their culture traits even while they adjust to life in the twentieth century.

Anthropologists studying the American Indians noticed that many culture traits were shared by tribes spread over a large area. The Haida, for instance, were only one of a group of tribes who had totem poles and potlatches, as well as oceangoing canoes of a particular type, long wooden houses, similar legends, a certain type of mask and so on. These tribes lived in Oregon, Washington, British Columbia, southern Alaska, and the offshore islands nearby. The geographical region in which similar living patterns show up is called a culture area.

The first floor of the Museum of the American Indian is devoted to Northern Woodlands, Great Lakes, Plains, Great Basin-Plateau and Southeast culture areas. On the second floor the Eskimo, Northwest Coast, Southwest and California culture areas are represented. Here also you can see some of the things archeologists have uncovered throughout the country that tell us of the life of the Indians before the white man came.

On the third floor there is rich proof that Central and South America and the West Indies produced a wide range of Indian ways of life. These countries also are divided into culture areas. One display is labeled "The Little People of Middle America." It is a village scene, made up of tiny clay figurines, each 1,000 years old. They were found in Mexico and Central America. Scientists are still not sure why these little figures were made. But the miniature children at play, women preparing food and holding their babies and priests with their elaborate headdresses conducting ceremonies have an indescribable charm.

As you leave the museum, you may want to stop at the sales desk, where you will find an excellent selection of books about Indian life, customs and history. You may also want to buy a piece of pottery, a ring or a piece of leather- or beadwork, made by Indians of today or yesterday.

Clay figures from Mexico and Central America

23

SAN DIEGO ZOO
Balboa Park
San Diego, California 92112

A few years ago, when the San Diego Zoo gave a party to celebrate its fiftieth birthday, two enormous birthday cakes decorated with frosted elephants and apes were served to more than 30,000 people and several chimpanzees. That's the kind of place the zoo is.

It's a good idea to begin with the zoo bus ride that takes you up and down, in and out through the three deep canyons that break up the otherwise flat mesa land of the zoo's 128 acres in Balboa Park. Your driver will point out the African lion grotto, the rain forest, the reptile house and other tempting places. You can come back later to those that interest you most.

Polar bear and cub

When your bus passes the bear grottoes, the driver will stop and call out to bears who are waiting there just to entertain you. One will wave, another begs; one salutes, and one puckers up as if to whistle. The polar bears raise their hands in a prayerful gesture. Every performer is rewarded with pieces of bread thrown by the driver. When a new cub makes his first public appearance, at the age of a few months, he soon learns that he will get a slice of bread if he is clever enough to lift up a paw or stand on his toes. Bears are natural actors who enjoy performing their tricks, and the drivers encourage any new act.

San Diego's birds are almost as popular as the bears, because of the imaginative way in which they are exhibited. A flying cage for tropical birds is 90 feet high. This is a cage *you* can get into. You enter near the top, and walk along a ramp that zigzags down through lush tropical foliage, as brightly plumed birds fly over your head. In another exhibit an arched doorway hung with strands of green beads leads into a glass-walled hummingbird enclosure. It is crowded with trees, and the feeling of dense foliage is increased

158

by hanging plants. Also hanging are troughs of water and nectar. Hummingbirds of more than twenty species dart back and forth, enjoying more flying space than they would have in any conventional cage. Sunlight shining through the glass makes them glitter like jewels in motion. Some varieties, such as the brown **Inca**, native to Colombia in South America and to the western part of Ecuador, are so tame they may sit on your shoulder.

A favorite part of the zoo is the koala sanctuary. The little creatures from Australia look like furry gray baby teddy bears. But the koala is a marsupial, with a pouch for carrying the young, more closely related to the kangaroo than to the bear.

When it is born, a baby koala is less than an inch long, and the mother carries it in her pouch until it is about eight months old. Finally, when the baby becomes so big that the mother can't carry it in her pouch anymore, she takes it on her back. Koalas grow to only about two feet in height; the males may be a little taller. They sleep most of the day. Their favorite foods are eucalyptus leaves and shoots.

San Diego's koalas arrived some years ago. Fortunately the San Diego Zoo has a remarkable botanical garden, including about thirty varieties of eucalyptus. After trying them all out, the koalas found nine or ten kinds of leaves they particularly liked, and so their food is homegrown. After a period of adjustment, they

Koala bear and cub

had settled into their new home well enough to begin producing young.

The San Diego Zoo is one of the few places outside Australia where these appealing little creatures are thriving. A group of koalas that the San Francisco Zoo had been lucky enough to obtain had to be transferred to San Diego when it became apparent that they did not feel enough at home to begin breeding.

A zoo gets its animals in many ways. Among the first animals to join the zoo in San Diego was a mountain lion that had been found by a rancher. Another was a Kodiak bear that a sailor raised from the time it was a cub until it grew to be bigger than the sailor. Other early animal inhabitants had been in Hollywood movies and were given to the zoo when they were no longer needed for films. But often the zoo goes out and hunts for its own specimens.

A few years ago Clyde Hill, an associate curator at San Diego, went to Madagascar on a field trip to search for strange animals native to that island off the coast of Africa. One of the rarities he was looking for was a sifaka, one variety of lemur. Lemurs are primates, like monkeys, apes and man. They are more primitive than monkeys. Their long tails are not prehensile (able to grasp branches or hold food) like those of some monkeys. Lemurs live in treetops, and have large, bright eyes. They are found only on Madagascar and a few nearby islands.

Curator Hill was joined in his search by a French scientist from the University of Madagascar, who served as interpreter. Together they set out for the inland village of Tsaramandrose. As soon as they arrived, the French professor spoke to the village children and asked them to bring in all the small animals they could find. The children quickly came back with a variety of lizards, including several kinds of chameleon. Then the scientists spoke to the village officials, who promised to help them capture sifakas and other lemurs the next day.

When morning came, they were joined by a government ranger

and a group of foresters. They selected a clearing in the forest for the center of the hunt. The sifakas and other animals would be captured there. The ranger organized the foresters and village men into several small scouting parties and sent them deep into the woods surrounding the clearing, where he and the two scientists would wait. When a scouting party located a sifaka, they were to drive the animal to the clearing by shouting and beating on tin cans. Because it was winter and all the leaves had fallen to the ground, the sifakas could easily be spotted as they swung through the trees.

Soon the waiting men heard a faint noise, which gradually became louder. Minutes later they saw a sifaka jumping from tree to tree until it reached one at the edge of the clearing. As it came closer to them, the men stopped their noisemaking. Silently they formed a large semicircle around the clearing practically surrounding the animal. It was trapped. It leaped to the ground and began to run with long, fast strides. But the men raced after it, and soon one of them scooped it up.

Two days of this hunting rewarded Curator Hill with five sifakas, three lemurs of other varieties and various reptiles. They were all packed into crates, boxes and sacks for the long trip home. The sifakas were friendly creatures, and in less than twenty-four hours were tame enough to sit in Hill's lap and eat from a spoon. Back in San Diego, they joined their cousins in the monkey quadrangle. They are the first of this type of lemur to be exhibited in an American zoo.

Another rare primate you can see in San Diego is the proboscis monkey, named for its very large hooked nose. Sometimes the nose curves around below the monkey's chin. A few years ago a young female named Honey Ong arrived. Until she came, two others named Penelope and Pinocchio had been the only proboscis monkeys in the Western Hemisphere. In Indonesia they live in the tops of mangrove trees high above swamps and rivers.

161

Honey Ong had been found by a forest ranger on the island of Borneo. She had fallen into a rushing river, where she was almost drowned before he rescued her. He sent her to Mrs. Barbara Harrisson, the wife of the director of the Sarawak Museum in Kuching, a city in the northwestern part of the island. Mrs. Harrisson, a naturalist who is very familiar with the primates of Borneo, hoped to return the little proboscis monkey to the wild. She wrote to the director of the zoo: "We will try to reintroduce her to a wild group but if this should fail (which is possible) I should like her to go to San Diego to join your two animals."

The first step in returning the animal to her natural habitat was to get her to accept living in a mangrove swamp. Only then could she slowly be brought near a small group of wild proboscis monkeys. Mrs. Harrisson tried twice to leave Honey Ong among the mangroves, but, as she wrote, "these attempts proved useless, as the animal is lost and terrified on its own." After the second try, when the little monkey suddenly dropped into the water below and started to swim out to sea, Mrs. Harrisson decided to give up. She wrote the end of the story: "I went after her and brought her back into captivity. She was named Honey for her color, Ong for her call."

About four months after she was rescued, Honey Ong arrived in San Diego, along with three rare Bornean earless lizards also sent by the Harrissons as a gift to the reptile department.

At San Diego's Children's Zoo young people can meet baby elephants, owls and bear cubs face to face. On Ape Island, part of the zoo, young orangutans and chimpanzees climb over and through an ultramodern piece of free-form playground equipment. On Spider Monkey Island the agile creatures can climb and swing by their prehensile tails from a set of elaborate monkey bars. The Seal Pool has two levels. At the top you may throw fish to the seals, and below you can put your eye to a porthole at water level and look one of the swimmers right in the eye.

162

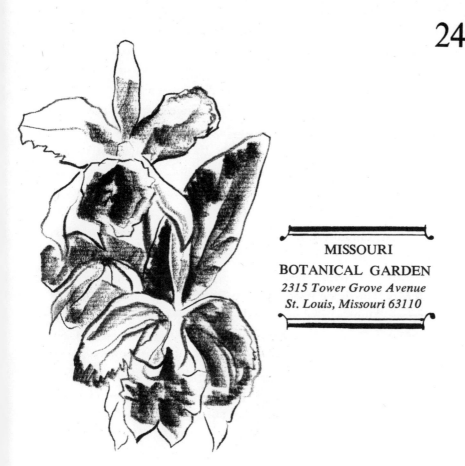

24

MISSOURI
BOTANICAL GARDEN
2315 Tower Grove Avenue
St. Louis, Missouri 63110

The city of St. Louis, on the Mississippi River, was beginning to be known as the Gateway to the West when a young man named Henry Shaw went into business there in the early nineteenth century. He was among the first to use the river as an inland water route for transporting goods from New Orleans instead of overland from the East. Explorers, fur traders and pioneer settlers all bought their provisions from him before venturing out into the wilds of the Louisiana Purchase Territory and beyond. He sold hatchets, knives and traps, imported from England, to fur traders and Indians. He also did a lively business in "tin plate"—dishes, cups and bowls of blue-enameled metal that could survive a trip West over rough trails. Henry Shaw made a fortune.

One of his friends was Dr. George Engelmann, a physician whose scientific interests had branched out from medicine to astronomy and botany. Engelmann was to become famous for his writings about plant life. He dreamed of someday having in St. Louis a place similar to Kew Gardens in London, where plants of almost every species were cultivated. They could be studied by scientists and enjoyed by the general public. Engelmann knew his friend Henry Shaw had the wealth that could make his dream come true.

Shaw had been born in England and had known Kew Gardens from his boyhood, when he attended school near London. Dr. Engelmann's research often took him across the Atlantic, and on one visit to Kew Gardens he persuaded its director, the famous British scientist Sir Joseph Hooker, to come to St. Louis and meet Mr. Shaw. Dr. Engelmann's dream began to come true.

Promising to provide both land and money for the Missouri Botanical Garden, Shaw sent Engelmann back to Europe to buy specimens and books for a reference library. Explorers heading West were asked to bring plants and seeds back to St. Louis when they returned. For thirty years Henry Shaw directed the garden, keeping its financial records, hiring scientists and gardeners and building up the collections.

Shaw's Garden, as everyone called it, was not the first in this country, but since the earlier ones did not last, it is the oldest. One of the first was founded in New York City by David Hosack. Like Dr. Engelmann, Hosack was both a physician and a botanist. In his day, this was a logical combination of interests. There were no drug manufacturers or drugstores as we know them today. Patent medicines, which might or might not be effective, were sold by traveling peddlers or in general stores. A conscientious physician had to provide the medicines he prescribed for his patients.

Hosack taught both medicine and botany at New York's Columbia University. For the benefit of his students as well as for himself, he decided to set up a garden "where plants useful to agriculture and medicine might be cultivated." In 1801, at his own expense, he bought 20 acres of land in the middle of Manhattan. But he found that the garden was too great an expense for him to keep up. Eventually the land in what was then a rural area went to Columbia University. As the growing city spread farther and farther north, the acreage became more and more valuable. Today, most of New York's famous Rockefeller Center stands on the land that was once Dr. Hosack's garden.

But Shaw's Garden survived and today the first thing you will notice is a building that looks like something one might well find at a world's fair. It is hard to believe that the sparkling clear plastic geodesic dome with its shining aluminum ribs is part of a botanical museum. This futuristic-looking structure is known as the Climatron. It is the air-conditioned, humidity-controlled home of thou-

Geodesic dome of the Climatron

sands of tropical plants. It has been called a jungle with walls. Plants that normally grow in South American, African and Asian jungles need plenty of moisture and sunlight. The clear plastic of the Climatron, unlike the shaded glass of the usual greenhouse, lets in all the light available.

Re-created inside the dome is the kind of tropical rain forest, complete with hills and bogs, that is found in equatorial zones all around the world. Rainfall in these areas is at least 100 inches a year, and may be as much as 450 inches. This quantity of moisture, plus the constant warm temperatures, produces lush foliage that is always green. Jungle trees do not drop their leaves all at once, as trees in Temperate Zone forests do. They lose a few leaves at a time, and new leaves are always growing at the top. Often the new growth is not green, but bright red.

The idea that a jungle is a tangle of low plants is inaccurate. Because jungle trees are always reaching up for more and more light, even the shortest are really very tall. Most are about 100 feet high, many reach 150 feet or more and even the lowest layer of vegetation averages about 25 feet. (Compare these figures to those for a Temperate Zone forest, in which the tallest trees are between 50 and 80 feet high, with a second tree layer 20 to 40 feet tall, and a low undergrowth only a few feet from the ground.)

Because most of the plants in the Climatron rain forest are very tall, a Gallery Walk was built from which you can look out at the topmost layer of vegetation. You get a whole new view of a tropical forest—a view that is never possible in a real jungle. From the Gallery Walk you can look down into a banana tree in flower, and get a closeup view of clusters of ripening fruit. You might find yourself facing into the branches of a royal palm or the light blue blooms of the bird-of-paradise. You can look straight out at a vine known as a strangler, growing in the angle where a branch comes out of a huge tree trunk. Its roots reach down the trunk of the host tree until they penetrate the soil. Then they become very large,

Jungle scene in Climatron

until they may completely encircle the trunk and perhaps kill the tree. Unlike parasites, which get food from their hosts, the strangler simply uses the host plant to give it a good "toehold." The strangler is called an epiphyte.

On one of the paths on the ground of the Climatron, you will find a waterfall splashing over real rocks into a pool 12 feet below. If you go on along this path, you find that it winds past rare, lush foliage, down to the bottom of the falls. Standing here, you feel cool, damp air blowing toward you just as you would if you were standing at the foot of a waterfall in a real rain forest. Among the stones in the pool is one that seems to float about. It is a piece of pumice, volcanic rock formed of lava. Because lava cools quickly, bubbles of gases and water vapor are trapped in the rock as it hardens. Then these spaces become filled with air. There is so much air in this stone that it is lighter than water, and it moves slowly about, astounding visitors until they discover the reason.

Across the Climatron is a larger pool containing tropical plants and fish. In its shallow end stands a clump of Egyptian paper plants. Papyrus, made from the stalks of this plant, was used as paper by the ancient Egyptians and gave us our word "paper."

A pathway leads on down to an aquatunnel under the pool. The tunnel's curved plastic roof forms part of the bottom of the pool. You can walk along in the tunnel and look up at fish and water lilies, a remarkable sight illuminated by underwater floodlights as well as by the natural light let in by the clear plastic walls of the Climatron.

When you come into the Climatron, you may notice an enormous instrument panel on your left. Here are the numerous devices with which an engineer and his assistants can make adjustments at any moment of the day or night. From this one panel, air temperature, air movement, water movement and lighting for every section of the building can be controlled separately. Two air-circulating systems, one for warm and the other for cool air, can be individually regulated to provide the ideal temperature for the plants. Twenty separate switches on the instrument panel control the exhaust fans that pull air through the building.

The Climatron is no little greenhouse. It is 70 feet high and 175 feet in diameter, and covers a ground surface of a bit more than half an acre. Because it was the first man-made jungle ever to be built anywhere, the Missouri botanists were unsure of just how effectively it could duplicate the natural tropical environment. But they soon learned that they needn't have worried. The climate control system worked so well that after only two years the jungle within walls looked like the real thing. Soon tropical plants grew so fast it became necessary to cut them back. Trimming off the extra growth of vines and trees when they get too big is an endless job. The trimmings have to be removed by the truckload!

Hibiscus blooms, African tulips and such tropical fruit trees as pineapple, papaya, mango and breadfruit are only a few of the plants to be seen. You can find sugarcane, chocolate trees, the vanilla orchid and the chewing gum tree (sapodilla)—from which we get ingredients for desserts and candies. Other interesting plants are the rubber tree, the manila hemp tree (rope is made of hemp) and the mahogany tree.

The Climatron is only one of the reasons for a visit to Shaw's Garden. Among the conventional greenhouses is one devoted exclusively to orchids. Beautiful outdoor plantings vary with the seasons. During the warm months, the roses and water lilies are spectacular.

Before you leave Mr. Shaw's Garden, visit Tower Grove, the house he lived in from 1849 until his death forty years later. Inside are the furnishings he placed there, including his piano. Cut flowers are in every room. The dining-room table is set as though a dinner party, like those he often gave, were about to take place.

An important part of any botanical garden is its collection of dead and preserved plant specimens. This is called an herbarium. The one in St. Louis contains about 2,000,000 plants from all over the world, including some brought back from the Antarctic by Admiral Byrd. Among botanists the 200,000-volume library of the Missouri Botanical Garden is famous. Many of its old and rare books were purchased by Dr. Engelmann, and many more were in his own library. Both the library and the herbarium are, for now, open only to scientific researchers. But when the new and larger building that is being planned becomes a reality, the public will be able to come and browse among the books and specimens.

25

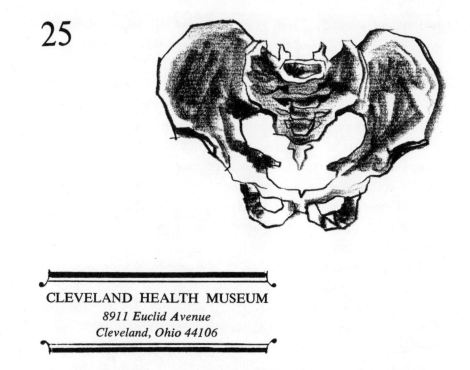

CLEVELAND HEALTH MUSEUM
8911 Euclid Avenue
Cleveland, Ohio 44106

Why would a museum appoint a Doctor of Medicine to be its director? Because that museum has taken on the job of teaching adults and children all it can about the world's greatest wonder— man himself. At the Cleveland Health Museum you can actually see into the human body. You can see how your brain works, how your blood flows, how your heart beats, how you grew to be a baby inside your mother and how you were born. You will get a clear, vividly illustrated explanation of the changes in your body that will turn you from a boy into a man or from a girl into a woman.

Let us begin with a transparent woman. She revolves on a wooden platform. Her skin is clear plastic and you can look right through it to an aluminum skeleton. Through the plastic you can also see red arteries, blue veins, nerves colored yellow and lymph glands green.

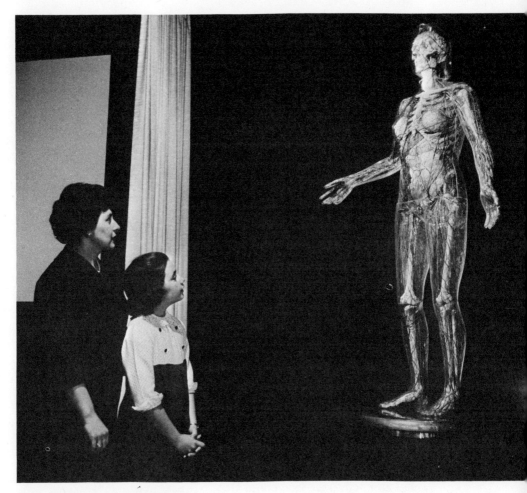

Juno, the transparent woman

She begins to talk. She asks you to observe her brain and the muscles of her voice box—called a larynx—with which she moves her vocal cords and produces speech. Then she tells of the other parts of the human body, and how they work together.

Elsewhere in the museum you may see how the process of digestion can change a hamburger, French fries and a milk shake into body tissue. You can find a clearly illustrated explanation of the chemical process by which we receive certain characteristics of our

171

parents even before we are born. Or you can spend fourteen minutes watching a remarkable demonstration of how the human brain works. There is no other exhibit like this one anywhere.

The huge, electronically operated brain does not look at all real, but its purpose is not to duplicate your brain's appearance. This gigantic model has 40 miles of wiring built into it, and 45,000 lights. It is 25 feet wide, 20 feet deep and 12 feet high. It shows you what staggeringly complicated things happen inside your brain every time you see and hear something and store it away to be remembered. The fourteen-minute demonstration shows what would happen during a single moment if you were at a concert watching a singer and listening to her song.

Two blue circles up front near the floor represent eyes. Two similar disks facing sideways represent ears. The rest of the model consists of disks of varying sizes, balls and connections. Patterns of light and the projection of pictures help show how sight and sound are received and transmitted. As complicated as the mechanism is, the way a brain functions becomes wonderfully clear. This is one of the most dramatic museum demonstrations of any kind in the country. The Upjohn Company, which manufactures drugs and medical supplies, had this exhibit made for the New York World's Fair, where millions of people came to see it in 1964 and 1965. An artist, Will Burton, designed it with the help of many scientists. It was given to the Cleveland Health Museum in 1966.

Cleveland's museum was the first of its kind in America. It was established in 1940, when doctors and educators began to realize that health could be improved by giving people a better understanding of their own bodies. Since then similar museums have been started in Dallas; Hinsdale, Illinois; Philadelphia; and at the Mayo Clinic in Rochester, Minnesota.

Part IV

SOME VERY SPECIAL PLACES

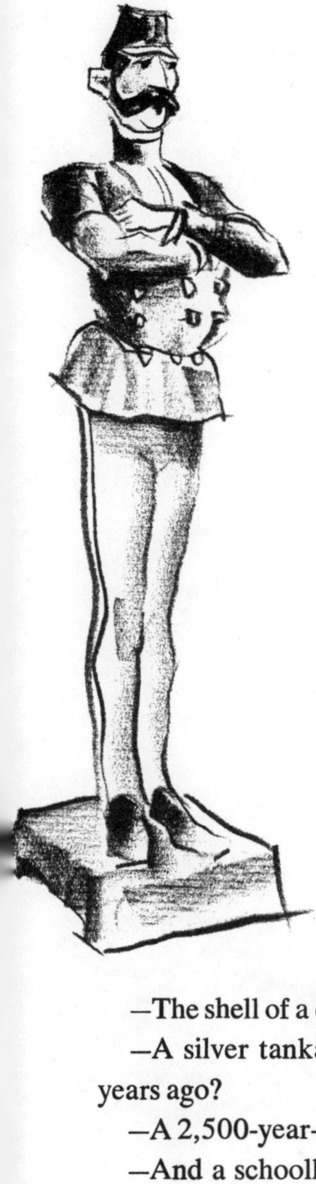

26

THE NEWARK MUSEUM
43-49 Washington Street
Newark, New Jersey 07101

Where would you go to find these treasures?

—Paintings by the eighteenth-century American artists Ralph Earl, John Singleton Copley, James Peale?

—Paintings by the twentieth-century Americans John Sloan, Edward Hopper, Joseph Stella?

—The shell of a chambered nautilus?

—A silver tankard made by a Dutch New Yorker almost 300 years ago?

—A 2,500-year-old coin from China?

—And a schoolhouse built when George Washington was President?

Would you go to six different places? Not if you happened to be in Newark, New Jersey. You could find them all at the Newark Museum.

The museum began more than 50 years ago in two rooms in the city's library. There librarian John Cotton Dana used to exhibit paintings, minerals, animal skeletons and other art and science collections that belonged to residents of Newark. One man had been to Japan, and brought back works by great artists of that country, as well as many other beautiful and strange objects. At that time —it was 1908—few people anywhere in America were familiar with Oriental art and handicrafts. People stared and were delighted by delicate paintings, elaborate ornaments for ceremonial swords and lovely little lacquered boxes. No one had ever seen anything like the impressive robe of dark-blue silk woven with gold threads that had once been worn by a Japanese actor.

Soon it was decided to establish a "Museum for the reception and exhibition of articles of art, science, history and technology." That was in 1909.

The city purchased the Oriental collection that had started the museum idea, and presented it to the new organization. Other collections were purchased or donated. But the growing museum remained in the library until 1926, when a new building was provided by department store owner Louis Bamberger.

John Cotton Dana became the first director, and he turned out to be an energetic leader who could excite the community and build its collections. He became famous among museum people throughout the country for his new ideas about what a museum should do. He dreamed of a place for "pleasure, enjoyment and knowledge," where visitors would become, in his words, "happier" as well as "wiser." Under Dana, Newark's museum became the first in the country to offer special courses to train future museum workers. He pioneered in exhibiting the paintings and sculptures of contemporary American artists. He was the first in the country to show industrial arts—that is, well-designed manufactured articles. He held an exhibit of German metal, wood and glass products, and of German textiles. A few years later he proved that good design was not too expensive for anyone to buy. He put together a show of objects found in five-and-ten-cent stores in the city. And after that he held the first exhibit devoted to one of the state's major industries.

Forty-two companies contributed to a show called "New Jersey's Clay Products," which explained step by step how pottery is manufactured and traced the history of pottery making. The first commercial pottery in the nation was made in Burlington, New Jersey, in 1684. The state has been a center of ceramics manufacture ever since. Most of the early products were useful but not especially pretty—bricks, tiles, table and cooking ware. But in time New Jersey turned out dinnerware fine enough for the White

House. The artisan who produced it, Walter Scott Lenox, had learned his craft as an apprentice in a Trenton factory. He became manager there, and hoped someday to have his own company and create ceramic pieces that would be both beautiful and practical. In particular, he dreamed of duplicating a kind of ware made in the town of Belleek, in Ireland. This is a thin china with a pearly white glaze, shaped into elaborate, dainty pieces.

In the 1880's Lenox got his chance, and formed the company that later bore his name. He hired two potters who had worked at the Irish factory, and he succeeded in producing pieces that many people think were even more beautiful than the original Belleek. One of his earliest and loveliest was a pitcher in the shape of a snail shell with a cupid sitting on top of it. Lenox gave the Newark Museum thirty-one pieces of his porcelain. The pitcher was not one of them, but it was purchased by the museum years later.

Some artists work in paint on canvas, some with clay, and some with needle and thread or yarn. Embroidery is an ancient art. Hundreds of years ago lengths of heavy fabric, sewn with colorful pictures or designs, were hung on the walls of stone buildings as a protection against cold and drafts and as a decoration too. Newark's decorative arts gallery has an embroidery that hung in an Italian cathedral in the seventeenth century. It shows the "Adoration of the Shepherds," who have come with their gifts for the newborn Baby Jesus. A decorative border embroidered around the scene frames it, and the complete hanging is 12½ feet high and nearly 14 feet wide.

In recent years artists with needle and thread have been making wall hangings for today's buildings, but these works are intended only as decorations. One of the first to rediscover the art of the wall hanging was Mariska Karasz, whose embroidery of an "Herb Garden" is in Newark. Miss Karasz had learned traditional stitches as a child in Hungary, and used them on the women's and children's clothing she designed when she came to this country. Then

178

Embroidered hanging
"Herb Garden"
by Mariska Karasz

she was asked to write a book about embroidery. The first time she picked up her needle and thread to create designs for her book, she realized that a whole new kind of embroidery was waiting to be discovered. She saw, as she said, that "the stitches can be made to sing out as words sing in a poem." And she began to create some extraordinary things with her needle. She used all sorts of fibers for thread—silk and wool, fishing line, tinsel and even cord. The color or texture of a piece of fabric would suggest a mood to her, and she would place threads against this background fabric in different ways until a theme and design came to her. Then she began to sew, inventing new stitches and building her patterns as she worked.

179

In addition to ceramics and wall hangings the decorative arts galleries at Newark also contain such different things as furniture, silver pieces, quilts, carpenters' tools, jewelry and armor.

At the time the Newark Museum was founded, there was only one art museum in New York City just across the Hudson River. That, of course, was the great Metropolitan Museum of Art. Obviously, Newark couldn't compete with this wealthy institution. Instead, the new museum chose to specialize in a subject that was not covered by any gallery in the larger city. It chose American art from Colonial days to the present. Since then several New York museums, devoted to different periods of American art, have come on the scene. But for a collection that shows the complete range of work in this country, even the New York art critics cross the river to Newark.

"Washington Under the Council Tree" was painted by Joseph Pickett, a carpenter who never left his native village of New Hope, Pennsylvania. He was untaught, or rather self-taught. He began painting when he was sixty-five, because he wanted to picture the history of his hometown. In the four years before he died in 1918 he produced some wonderful scenes that are now in our museums.

New Hope was George Washington's headquarters before his famous crossing of the Delaware River, the maneuver that was to give him his first real military success in the War of Independence. Pickett worked with very thick paint, and made it even stiffer by adding gravel and bits of ground-up shell. As a result, the trunk of the tree and other forms in the picture stand out from the background.

Self-taught artists such as Pickett—known as primitives—have been painting the American scene since the days of the earliest settlements. Newark has many of their works, including Edward Hicks' painting of "The Grave of William Penn." Unlike Pickett, Hicks was a painter all his life. He painted signs, furniture and wagons as well as pictures of religious or historic scenes. He is best known for almost sixty views of an imaginary country known as "The Peaceable Kingdom," where all the birds and beasts were supposed to live together as friends.

Newark takes great pride in its collection of objects from Tibet. The museum's interest in the small mountain country goes back to 1911, when a trustee met a missionary doctor returning from Asia. When the trustee learned of the magnificent and unusual collection the doctor had brought from Tibet, he immediately began to plan how it might join the Japanese group already in the museum.

"Washington Under the Council Tree"

His vision of an important Oriental gallery was eventually realized. In later years more Tibetan articles were acquired, until there are now about 2,000 in a collection that is priceless. Silk wall hangings, religious objects hammered out of pure silver, costumes, musical instruments, religious books and even a tent make up an unusual record of life in a land rarely visited by outsiders.

From neighboring Nepal comes one of the newest additions to the Oriental collection. It is a round medallion known as a mandala that was intended for the ceiling of a temple. It is 35 inches in diameter, and set with hundreds of tiny jewels arranged in

Mandala

Tibetan Wheel of the Law

concentric circles. This design represents various deities and the order of their importance.

The Oriental collection includes also fine works from India, China and Korea.

If you are a coin collector, you won't want to miss the outstanding numismatic exhibits. Among them are an almost complete range of United States coins, including money used in Colonial days and a very rare silver dollar minted in 1804. There is ancient Chinese bronze money in the shape of both a bell and a knife, and there are gold coins from Byzantium.

In the science galleries are displays devoted to anthropology, biology and geology. An excellent collection of more than 1,000 shells includes unusual tropical ones with such strange names as bear's paw clam, Triton's trumpet, Turk's cap and melon shell. A unique display shows plants that are used for food, medicine and other practical purposes.

The physics exhibit illustrates the basic principles of mechanics —the way simple machines work. Hundreds of tiny parts move to show the action of levers, pulleys, inclined planes and gears. In other exhibits you can learn about electricity, examine live animals and watch a planetarium show.

Before you leave, visit the schoolhouse in the garden. It was built in 1784, and still contains the desks and benches, quill pens and hornbooks, old stove and dunce stool used by the schoolmaster and his pupils long, long ago.

185

Stainless-steel sculpture by contemporary American sculptor David Smith

27

THE FARMERS' MUSEUM,
THE VILLAGE CROSSROADS,
AND FENIMORE HOUSE
Lake Road
Cooperstown, New York 13326

NATIONAL BASEBALL
HALL OF FAME AND MUSEUM
Main Street
Cooperstown, New York 13326

INDIAN MUSEUM
1 Pioneer Street (P.O. Box 123)
Cooperstown, New York 13326

WOODLAND MUSEUM
Lake Road (P.O. Box 392)
Cooperstown, New York 13326

These words were written by a lawyer, William Cooper:

In 1785 I visited the rough and hill country of Otsego, where there existed not an inhabitant, nor any trace of a road; I was alone, three hundred miles from home, without bread, meat, or food of any kind; fire and fishing tackle were my only means of subsistence. I caught

186

trout in the brook and roasted them on the ashes. My horse fed on the grass that grew by the edge of the waters. I laid me down to sleep in my watch coat, nothing but the melancholy wilderness around me. In this way, I explored the country, formed my plans for future settlement, and meditated upon the spot where a place of trade or a village should afterwards be established.

The following year William Cooper returned to the country around Otsego Lake in upper New York State to found the settlement that bears his name. To it came farmers who tamed the wilderness, and artisans who provided goods and services.

Within a few years there were several frame houses and barns, a store, a tannery and a smithy. Cooperstown became the county seat of Otsego County, and its founder became the first judge of the county court. A courthouse and jail went up; then a tavern. More settlers arrived and built stores and houses. Two lawyers and two doctors were attracted by the growing community. In 1793 the first school was opened. Two years later came the first newspaper and the first clergyman. The settlers established mills and a public library. They built roads. And, in 1805, the community erected its first church. The pioneers worked hard, and built a lovely town.

Cooperstown was a fine place to grow up in. Of course there were chores to be done. But there was still plenty of time for wandering through the woods, playing on the shores of the lake, staring at mountains often hidden in mist, listening to stories told by older men, coming to know Indians who lived nearby.

Judge Cooper's youngest son, James Fenimore, did all these things. He was to become America's first great novelist and first famous author. In his many books he told stories set in the countryside where he lived as a boy.

Today Cooperstown is still a charming village. Somehow it stays serene despite the hordes of visitors who come every year to its four museums.

Entrance to the Farmers' Museum

Begin your tour at the Farmers' Museum, which is in a large old barn. First you will see the implements and other personal possessions of a pioneer family. Most of these things were handmade. The farmer, aided by neighbors or relatives, built his own house and barn. One exhibit shows you how he did it. The skills needed to provide the necessities of life are demonstrated by museum workers. Watch as the woodworker smooths and shapes, cuts and whittles to produce simple farm tools and furniture. Watch the broommaker tying bundles of coarse straw with the aid of a simple machine. Watch linen yarn being spun from flax, wool yarn from sheep's wool. The yarn is woven into rough cloth; the cloth is sewn by hand to make all the garments worn by the family. An exhibit called "The Farmer's Year" explains how jobs on the farm varied from month to month as the season changed. Even in winter, when little could be done outdoors, the farmer was busy—repairing his tools, fashioning new equipment for use in the months ahead. As you touch the worn handle of a grain shovel or feel the coarse texture of homespun cloth, you can imagine what it was like to live in those days, using those tools, wearing garments of that cloth.

Leave the Farmers' Museum and walk along the street named the Village Crossroads. A group of small buildings, all about 150 years old, have been moved here from villages in the surrounding area. In each a staff member is waiting to explain what the building was used for, to demonstrate equipment and to answer your questions.

In the Blacksmith's Shop you will find the smith at his glowing

forge. You watch him heat and bend the strong metal. Perhaps you will see him shoe a horse or an ox from the farm down the road. The smith also fashioned every household and farm implement that could be made from iron. You can handle his tools and his wrought-iron work.

At the Country Store you can buy penny candy—licorice, rock candy, peppermint sticks. Oil lamps and buckets hang from the walls and ceiling. Straw hats, china teacups and other goods fill the shelves. Farmers would come from outlying areas to exchange their produce for things that couldn't be made or grown on the farm—patent medicines, spices, coffee, tea. This general store, with its narrow benches and stools pulled up to the stove for warmth, a checker game set up on a barrel nearby, was a center of gossip and fellowship.

Along the Village Crossroads there is also a druggist's shop, where such things as herbal remedies and perfumes were concocted and sold. An herb garden, producing ingredients for medicines, grows between the shop and the doctor's office. Nearby is the law office of Samuel Nelson, a country lawyer who became a Justice of the United States Supreme Court.

The Bump Tavern is a typical turnpike inn of its period. It was built in 1800, but is named for a later owner, Ephraim Bump, who enlarged it and added front porches. With a ladies' parlor, gentlemen's reading room, ballroom and other facilities, it was a place for social gatherings as well as a home away from home for travelers.

There are also a one-room schoolhouse, a wagon shed and a carriage shed. In the printing office a weekly newspaper is still being turned out. In the little church at the end of the street, nondenominational services are held every Sunday afternoon. A log cabin once used by a trapper, and still furnished with traps and hunting gear, is set in the woods back from the street.

On your walk along the Village Crossroads you may visit a real working farm. In the barnyard, surrounded by a low fence, are

190

farm animals—chickens, ducks, pigs, a few sheep, a team of oxen, a cow—just what an average homesteader would have owned. Most of them have the run of the grounds, and you may find the sheep grazing near the farmhouse instead of behind it in the barnyard. Corn, flax and other crops are grown on the farm. Chores are still performed daily. Cows must be milked and eggs collected. Seeds are sown, plants tended and crops harvested. In the fall, hay is stacked near the barn.

In the farmhouse itself, visitors like to linger in the large kitchen. Here the museum worker, acting as the farmwife, may be churning butter, making cheese, cooking in the open brick fireplace or baking bread in the oven built in next to it. The farm's cow and chickens provide the milk and eggs used for cooking, and if you happen to be visiting when the bread comes out of the oven, you will be given a warm, delicious slice.

Your next stop is at Fenimore House, the large ivy-covered building with four white pillars at its entrance. It contains an unusually fine collection of American folk art—paintings, sculpture and crafts produced by self-taught artists. There are many portraits of townspeople—people who might have lived or worked in any of the buildings you have just seen along the Village Crossroads. These people made, or ordered from talented craftsmen, the sort of embroideries, wood carvings, paintings of familiar scenes, portraits of family members, weather vanes, patriotic signs and toys exhib-

ited here. In addition, Fenimore House displays memorabilia of the Cooper family, especially of James Fenimore Cooper. It is also the headquarters of the New York State Historical Association, which maintains the Farmers' Museum, the Village Crossroads and Fenimore House.

A favorite American sport, baseball, was invented in Cooperstown in 1839. At the age of twenty, Abner Doubleday, who later became a famous Union general during the Civil War, laid out a diamond-shaped playing field in a cow pasture. One hundred years later the National Baseball Hall of Fame and Museum was established at Cooperstown. On display are mementos of famous players and historic games, including Doubleday's own baseball. There

Vincent Civiletti painting from Hall of Fame

are photographs of each President since William Howard Taft throwing out the first ball for the American League team in Washington, and the baseball each has autographed. You can follow the steps in the manufacture of balls, bats and gloves, or spend hours memorizing the statistics of major league games and players posted on one wall. The uniforms of such baseball greats as Babe Ruth and Lou Gehrig are here, along with the home plate and cornerstone from the old Ebbets Field, home of the Brooklyn Dodgers. A reference library holds the answer to any question about scores and records.

In recent years local residents have added two new museums to tell other parts of the area's story. Clyde Olson is the director of the Cooperstown Indian Museum. He is a self-taught and highly competent archeologist. He has used his collection of artifacts, some of them 10,000 years old, to create scenes from Indian life and history in this part of the state. When he began to plan an Indian display, the New York State Historical Association also gave him material from its collection.

Louis B. Hager is the director of the Woodland Museum, which tells the story of James Fenimore Cooper and the countryside he loved. One building is devoted to Cooper, and displays scenes from his most famous novel, *The Deerslayer.* You may walk around a 40-foot relief map of the Otsego Lake region, where the action of the novel takes place. The water in the map's lake is real, and a real waterfall drops over real rocks. Outside, you may walk along paths winding through the forest and find more than 100 varieties of wild flowers and trees, all of them labeled. You may ride on a horse-drawn trolley around a circle of track, or on a two-car railroad train pulled through the forest by an antique engine. Another building is devoted to the wild animal life of the area.

It would be difficult to see all these places and enjoy the beauty of the Otsego Lake area in one day. It is a good idea to spend two days or even three.

28

BUFFALO BILL MUSEUM
Buffalo Bill Historical Center
836 Sheridan Avenue (P.O. Box 1262)
Cody, Wyoming 82414

WHITNEY GALLERY
OF WESTERN ART
Buffalo Bill Historical Center
720 Sheridan Avenue (P.O. Box 1020)
Cody, Wyoming 82414

"THE BRONCO BUSTER" BY FREDERIC REMINGTON

The city of Cody is a small one. Only about 5,000 people live here. But hundreds of thousands of visitors come here every year. For Cody is located right on the highway that leads to the East Entrance of Yellowstone National Park.

As you drive down a street in the center of town, you see the Rocky Mountains towering in the distance. At the end of the street, just at the edge of town, rises a larger-than-life-size statue of a man on a horse. The man is in cowboy gear, and his rifle points into the air. The horse rears, raising his head to the sky above. The statue is called "Buffalo Bill, the Scout."

The man known as Buffalo Bill was a national hero when he was still a teen-age boy. He was born in Iowa and named William Frederick Cody. His father died when the boy was only thirteen

"William F. Cody" by Rosa Bonheur

and from then on he had to support his family. He worked for supply trains and a freighting company. Two years later young Bill Cody was digging for gold in Colorado, and the following year, at the age of sixteen, he rode for the Pony Express. During the Civil War and for several years afterward he was chief of scouts for the U.S. Army. He served with Generals Miles, Sheridan, Custer and others, leading their troops through the unfamiliar wilderness, carrying important messages through difficult and hostile country and helping plan attacks on Indian encampments. He knew which red men could be treated as friends and which could not. He earned the title of Colonel, and received the Congressional Medal of Honor for his services.

In between his years of military activity he was a buffalo hunter, supplying meat to the construction crews of the Kansas Pacific Railroad, which was being built across the plains. After it was reported that he had slain 4,000 head of buffalo in little more than a year, his fame spread throughout the country, and he had a nickname.

Then he went on the stage, to star in a play about his career, written by an admirer. Audiences were so enthusiastic about his authentic Western style that he was encouraged to organize his own, really Western, show. For fifteen years Buffalo Bill's Wild West Show traveled about the country. It crossed the Atlantic a dozen times. His troupe included more than 500 cowboys and Indians, along with their wild broncos and a herd of live buffalo. Everyone flocked to see these Westerners and the famous Indian chiefs, Sitting Bull and Red Coud, and the sharpshooting young girl Annie Oakley.

In the last twenty years of his life, Buffalo Bill became a ranch owner in Wyoming, where he founded the town of Cody. After his death in 1917, the Buffalo Bill Memorial Association was formed by his neighbors and relatives and friends all over the country, to keep his memory alive and to save what they could of the real

Wild West for future generations. Today this association maintains the two museums of the Buffalo Bill Historical Center.

The center is located on a 40-acre site at the edge of Cody, just off the highway leading to Yellowstone. The statue of the hero on his favorite horse, sculpted by Mrs. Gertrude Vanderbilt Whitney (founder of New York's Whitney Museum), was the first exhibit.

Your visit might begin at the small two-story wood house that was his boyhood home. It was built about 1840 in Iowa, six years before he was born. It was moved to its present location almost 100 years later, and filled with family possessions and furniture of the period. Nearby is a large log cabin that is a duplication of Cody's home on his ranch a few miles outside town.

At the new Buffalo Bill Museum building you can examine the rich collection devoted to the Western hero. Here are his guns and garments, medals and trophies. Here are photographs, posters and pictures of his Wild West Show; gifts from European royalty; saddles and other gear; flags he served under; and Indian blankets and jewelry that were given him. There are also dozens of Indian arrowheads, many elaborate and beautifully beaded costumes worn by Indians of the Great Plains, war bonnets and scalps, and artifacts from prehistoric Indian settlements of the area.

Here, also, you will come upon two stagecoaches that were part of Buffalo Bill's Wild West Show. These were originally Deadwood Stages, running between the towns of Deadwood, South Dakota, and Cheyenne, Wyoming. One of them, now painted bright red with yellow wheels and black trim, had been captured and partially burned by hostile Indians before Cody acquired it. He refurbished it and used it for the opening parade of his show. When the show traveled to Europe, this stage went along too, and at least five royal persons rode in it.

The animal that gave Cody his famous nickname is well remembered at the museum. Many pictures of buffalo and the hunt are on the walls. There are skulls of animals that were left on the plains and bleached white by sun and wind and rain. You will also see an impressive collection of things made by Indians from buffalo hide, including an elaborately painted tepee.

Next door is the Whitney Gallery of Western Art, devoted to works by nineteenth-century artists who painted the West—its landscapes, wildlife and people.

One of them, a man who was more famous in his own day than in ours, was Albert Bierstadt. His were the first paintings of the majestic Rockies to be shown in the East. People thrilled to his enormous canvases filled with the dramatic shapes and vivid colors of the Western scene, and he became the most successful painter of his day. We can understand why when we look at "Wind River, Wyoming." Craggy heights are bathed in the yellow-gold of the setting sun, trees and lower hills glow darkly in red-brown shadows.

Charles M. Russell is known as the cowboy artist because he was indeed a part of the life he painted. Although self-taught, he was very skillful in his drawing of Indians. A portrait of a brave or a returning war party captures the strength and pride of a people who knew their way of life was about to change. "The Story Teller" is a painting of an aged brave recounting tribal legends to a group of women and children around the fire inside a tepee. The group listens intently, but one tot, too young to understand, plays idly with a doll.

Best known today of the Western artists is Frederic Remington. He painted every aspect of life in the Old West—tired horses and riders, Indians slaughtering a buffalo, soldiers resting and regrouping after battle. Remington was also a sculptor, and among his bronzes is "The Bronco Buster," a cowboy on the back of a wild horse.

These two buildings look out on one of the most spectacular views of any museum anywhere. In both of them, lounge areas with enormous picture windows have been built to take advantage of it. Past Mrs. Whitney's statue of Buffalo Bill rise the distant peaks of the Rocky Mountains, which change color as the day passes.

There can be little doubt that this is Buffalo Bill country for miles around. The highway to Yellowstone passes the Buffalo Bill Reservoir, which receives melting snow from the mountains and provides irrigation for the area. The reservoir is formed by the Buffalo Bill Dam, a project proposed by Colonel Cody back in 1905. In the days before power equipment, it was built by men, with mules and shovels. When it was completed five years later, it was the highest dam—328 feet—in the world.

"The End of the Trail" by James Earle Fraser

29

THE MARINERS MUSEUM
Museum Drive
Newport News, Virginia 23601

BALTIMORE AND OHIO
TRANSPORTATION MUSEUM
Pratt and Poppleton Streets
Baltimore, Maryland 21201

THE AIR FORCE MUSEUM
Wright-Patterson Air Force Base
Dayton, Ohio 45433

Would you like to climb into a round bullboat made of buffalo hide by an American Indian named Crow's Heart? To see the first American steam locomotive and the first American streamlined diesel? To walk through the fuselage of a fighter plane and examine the contents of its bomb bay?

The story of transportation tells much about how man conquered his world. Ships, trains and planes all conjure up visions of adventure. And the museums devoted to them tell an exciting and continuing story.

The Mariners Museum tells of ships and how they developed from sail to steam, how they were built and operated through the ages, from the most primitive rafts to the nuclear-powered vessels of today. As you approach the museum, you discover a collection of propellers, cannon and anchors spread out on the ground. Towering over them is a 12-foot statue of the Viking explorer Leif Ericsson, who is believed to have been the first European to sail across the ocean to North America, almost 500 years before Columbus' voyage. The statue, a symbol of man's conquest of the sea, is a copy of one presented to the people of Iceland by the United States.

Just inside the museum entrance is a large carved wood statue of Neptune, god of the sea to the ancient Romans. This particular Neptune was once a ship's figurehead. He is very much at home here, mounted on the wall between two carved sea horses.

More than eighty other figureheads hang high on the gallery walls. They seem to lean over you because they have been mounted at the angle at which they were attached to the bow of a ship. But the figurehead likely to catch your eye first is not on the wall. It is a giant gold-painted eagle. Because of its extraordinary

size—it has a wingspread of 18 feet and weighs more than 1½ tons—it stands at the center of the gallery. This eagle was made in 1880 for the steam frigate *Lancaster*.

Figureheads represented historical or mythological persons, or real or imaginary animals. Mermaids and Queen Victoria, the Russian Czar Alexander II and the American statesman Daniel Webster are in the collection. One of the more handsome beasts is the lion that once decorated the old iron British clipper ship *Derwent*. The lion is 12 feet high and was carved from teak, one of the hardest woods, in Scotland.

Below the figureheads are various exhibits. A sailmaker's bench, with a complete set of tools, is in front of a large picture of sails being fashioned by hand in a ship outfitter's factory. Nearby hangs a knot board, displaying about sixty different intricate sailor's knots. The knots were both practical and ornamental.

In the days of sailing ships, men at sea had a great deal of spare time. To while away the hours, they used the materials at hand to make decorative or useful things. Rope and cord were always plentiful on board ship. Literally thousands of different knots and splices were worked out by sailors, who used them to make all sorts of cord-worked things. They made ditty bags to carry their personal gear; weather cloths, gangway and stern-sheet covers, belts, purses, handles for sea chests and bellpulls.

Carving was another favorite pastime. Cups, small boxes and trinkets were fashioned out of scrap wood or driftwood. And ships were carved to fit into bottles. Their masts and sails were hinged so that they could be dropped when the ship was being put into the bottle, and pulled up taut afterward.

Scrimshaw is the name given to carvings made from whale teeth, bone and ivory. Whaling journeys might last two years or more, with little for the men to do for long periods of time. Sailors polished whale teeth and etched them with nautical scenes and pictures copied from magazines. They carved chessmen, ivory tool

DESIGNS
OF THE TATTOOERS ART

handles, decorative boxes, paper knives, canes and, surprisingly, rolling pins and pastry crimpers, presents for the womenfolk at home.

A unique display is built around objects that came from a waterfront tattooing parlor in Norfolk, Virginia. A sailor was expected to have one or more permanent tattooed designs somewhere on his body. You can see the inks and lotions, and hand and electric needles that were actually used. A statuette of a man completely covered with multicolored markings is a great advertisement for the tattooer's art. Customers selected designs they wanted from sample sheets.

In other exhibits at the Mariners Museum are models used to recreate famous naval events. A favorite with visitors depicts the Civil War battle between the *Monitor* and the *Merrimack*. These vessels, called ironclads, were covered with iron for protection in battle.

Another scene reconstructs the building of the first ship for which written instructions are available. The boat is, of course, Noah's Ark, and the precise measurements and specifications appear, in full detail, in the Bible.

The Mariners Museum is the place to find relics of famous vessels. A bronze bolt and a piece of ballast once belonged to the HMS *Bounty,* the ship made famous by the mutiny of its crew. These were found by the Mariners Museum on Pitcairn Island, where the *Bounty* was finally scuttled and burned and where her crew settled. The relics belonged to a descendant of Fletcher Christian, who had led the mutiny. They were obtained from him by barter. From the U.S. frigate *Constitution* there are pieces of her original oak hull, built in 1797, and copper rivets made by Paul Revere. From the schooner yacht *America,* for which the America's Cup race was named, there are pieces of spars and rigging. Her 10-foot cabin skylight has been made into a display case for other yachting exhibits.

Each one of a group of miniature ships represents a stage in the history of water transportation. These small models were precisely carved to scale. Each was built from the keel up, piece by piece, in exactly the way real ships are constructed. Every rope and tackle, every bit of rigging is accurately reproduced and in its proper place. Some details of these vessels are so small that magnifying glasses have been mounted in the display case through which each bit of carving can be seen. The height of nautical luxury is reached by a model of the galley that belonged to the French King Louis XIV. Even the oar blades are carved, and miniature figures toil on the deck, but you can really see them only through the magnifying glass.

A whole room is given over to navigational instruments—sextants, periscopes, chronometers, depth indicators, telescopes, signaling devices and so on. In the library are complete records of many shipbuilding companies, every book and magazine on sea-

French galley Madame

faring and the sea that you could want, thousands of photographs of ships and thousands of maps and charts. An art collection contains more than 10,000 prints and paintings of ships and shipbuilding and seafaring.

Most of the staff of the Mariners Museum have served at sea. The director is a retired U.S. Navy admiral.

Outside the museum is a beautiful park, with picnic areas, hiking trails and a freshwater lake stocked for fishing, with rowboats available. Near the museum building is a group of small boats. Here are dugouts, birchbark canoes, fishing boats of many countries, lifeboats, surfboats and small submarines. You may, if you like, go into all of them.

The first railroad for public transportation in the United States was the Baltimore and Ohio, which was founded in 1827. When construction began, the first stone was laid by the last living signer of the Declaration of Independence, John Carroll of Carrollton. He declared that, after the signing of the Declaration, this was the most important act of his life. He foresaw the extraordinary influence the railroad would have on the growth and development of the nation he had helped found.

By 1830 regular passenger service was begun. The first trains were very much like stagecoaches, with one big difference: The wheels ran along iron tracks. Because the wheels of the coach ran smoothly along tracks, with a minimum of friction, only one horse was needed to pull the load, instead of the team necessary for a stagecoach.

But steam power was already being used in England. Peter Cooper urged the B & O to use steam instead of horsepower, and he designed the first American locomotive. A steam boiler on it provided power which moved the locomotive's wheels by means of gears, and pulled other cars. It could run at speeds up to 18 miles an hour. When the first trains pulled by steam engines arrived at the new station at the foot of Capitol Hill, President Jackson and his whole Cabinet went over to watch the opening of the Washington line.

You enter the B & O's museum through the oldest railroad station in the world. Here the tickets for the first regularly scheduled horse-drawn passenger trains were sold. For a 26-mile round trip, the fare was seventy-five cents. The small building is of red brick with white trim. A bronze plaque to the left of the doorway tells its history briefly. To the right of the doorway another plaque tells about the first message ever sent by electric telegraph. Samuel F. B. Morse built his experimental telegraph line along the right-of-way, or route, of the B & O between Baltimore and Washington. On May 24, 1844, that first message, "What hath God wrought," was

206

Woodburning steam locomotive William Mason in the roundhouse

relayed between the Pratt Street B & O station in Baltimore and the Supreme Court chamber in the capital.

From the tiny station you enter an enormous roundhouse where actual historic locomotives and cars are displayed. This collection began when a B & O official, Major Pangborn, reconditioned some old cars for display at the Chicago World's Fair of 1893. Some of these were rusting away, hidden in corners of the road's shops and yards. Others had to be taken out of regular service to make the trip to Chicago; they were still working hard. Some had been for fifty years. But there were still other historic cars that could not be found. Among them was Peter Cooper's engine which had been nicknamed the Tom Thumb because of its small size. Major Pangborn did, however, locate the old record books, drawings and specifications, and built a new Tom Thumb just as it would have been built in 1830. This replica, which can be operated under its own steam, is now at the B & O Museum.

Also in the roundhouse is the John Hancock, the first locomotive with a cab for its engineer (1836); the Lafayette, first to have a horizontal boiler (1837); the Memnon, an early coal-burning engine that hauled supplies and troops in the Civil War (1848); and the first streamlined diesel locomotive to be operated in this country (1937).

The cars carried along by the locomotives are called rolling stock. On display are iron freight cars that were the ancestors of our all-steel or aluminum ones, and early boxcars and hoppers. Some of the more luxurious early passenger cars were still basically stage-coaches, with an upper deck protected only by an iron rail and covered with a sort of canopy. The passengers had a scenic but grimy ride.

All sorts of things interesting to railroad buffs can be found in still another part of the museum: old train schedules and tickets, lanterns, early systems of railroad communications, passenger car furnishings and nineteenth-century advertisements drawn by fine artists hired to do the job. Pieces of rail sections show how today's heavy-duty steel rails have gradually been developed to replace early lighter ones.

You will find also a collection of old-fashioned toy trains, and miniature locomotives and cars. Many of these tiny model trains were constructed with great accuracy and precision by M. D. Thornburgh, a longtime employee of the B & O. Some are literally priceless. Don't miss the elaborated model railroad setup in a setting of mountains and village, complete with several levels of track, and a railroad yard with storage tracks, a roundhouse and a turntable for car repair.

On December 17, 1903, Wilbur and Orville Wright successfully flew through the air in a power-driven machine of their own design. That historic flight took place at Kitty Hawk, North Carolina. In preparation for it the Wright brothers spent long hours of hard work in the repair shop of their bicycle business in Dayton, Ohio, the city that can now boast that it is the Birthplace of Aviation.

Some 12 miles outside Dayton, at the end of Main Street in the suburb of Fairborn, a glistening silver object stands 82½ feet high, pointing skyward. It is an Atlas intercontinental ballistic missile, designed to launch a nuclear warhead toward a far-distant target, and used as a booster for American spaceships. Although the Atlas is, through photographs and television, a familiar shape to everyone today, you will probably still be amazed when you see it up close in all its gleaming, gigantic splendor—a totem pole for the space age.

The first flight of the Wright brothers and the first American space launch were separated by only fifty-five years. The Air Force Museum, in front of which the Atlas stands, tells the history of aviation. In particular it spotlights the history, heritage and traditions of the United States Air Force. It is the world's largest military aviation museum. More than ninety military aircraft and missiles are on view, along with instruments, propellers, mementos of famous aviators, power systems, models and murals.

The world's first military heavier-than-air flying machine was a Wright design of 1909. Its maximum speed was 42 miles per hour, and its endurance in the air was about one hour. It weighed 740 pounds, and had a single four-cylinder engine. That original plane, Signal Corps Airplane No. 1, is now in the Smithsonian Institution in Washington. The Wright Military Flyer on display in Dayton is a duplicate, built at the Air Force Museum and fitted with the original engine, chains, sprockets and propellers donated by Orville Wright and members of his family.

The wings of a World War I plane on display have been stripped

209

of most of the fabric covering to show the wire-supported wooden construction used in those days. You can see how the body and wings of the plane were covered. All these early models were fabric-covered biplanes. There were two sets of wings, one above and one below the fuselage. The first metal-skinned monoplane was the Boeing P-26A of 1933.

Famous propeller planes used in World War II are the Boeing B-17, or Flying Fortress, and the heavier B-29 Superfortress. The B-29 on display is the plane that made the world's second atomic bomb raid, over Nagasaki, on August 9, 1945. The plane which has a wide mouth and sharp teeth painted just below its nose is a Curtiss P-40N Warhawk. It was made famous by the Flying Tigers, American volunteers who flew raids against the Japanese in China and Southeast Asia earlier in the war. The mouth and teeth represent the tiger shark.

Also from World War II days are England's Royal Air Force Spitfire, and German and Japanese fighter planes. All these propeller planes were as familiar twenty-five years ago as jet-propelled and rocket-powered aircraft, also on view, are today.

Inside a B-29's fuselage, you may inspect the controls, work stations and bombs. Also on display are the *Columbine,* the plane used by former President Eisenhower, and the B-52 *Lucky Lady III* which set a world speed record for a nonstop, round-the-world flight in 1957. There are uniforms, photographic equipment, a Russian MiG-15, and a display explaining the foods and feeding systems used on space flights.

If you want to take away a souvenir, stop as you leave the museum at the museum's sales desk to buy postcards, pennants or a model airplane kit.

30

THE JOHN WOODMAN HIGGINS ARMORY
100 Barber Avenue
Worcester, Massachusetts 01606

If you have ever dreamed about what it was like to be a knight at King Arthur's court, then come to Worcester, Massachusetts. Several dozen knights in full armor, with swords and lances at the ready, await you in the tall steel and glass building of a modern metalworking factory.

John Woodman Higgins, president of the Worcester Pressed Steel Company, recognized that the products made in his factory were related to the careful metalwork done by handcraftsmen hundreds of years ago. He began to collect fine examples of armor and other early metalwork. In 1931 he opened his museum, on the top two floors of his company's new building. The entrance is at one corner, and if you look way up to the roof before you go in, you will see a huge suit of armor.

As you enter the main exhibit area, two long corridors stretch out at an angle before you. The one on your left is called the Ancient Wing. Overhead fly banners and flags that once accompanied the noblemen of Europe into battle. The walls are of stone, with arched alcoves, windows and ceilings. Although this hall is not a reproduction of a medieval castle, it is designed to give you the feeling of one.

You will probably notice first the small suit of armor for a dog, standing in the middle of this gallery. Near it are metal outfits much smaller than those of the knights ranged along the walls. These were worn by the young assistants who accompanied every knight, boys who would someday become knights.

Preparation for knighthood was long and difficult. For the son of a nobleman it might begin at the age of seven, when he would leave his father's house and go to the castle of a higher-ranking nobleman. Or he might go to serve the king. At the castle these young boys, known as pages or varlets, were instructed in religion and court etiquette. They performed such tasks as carving roast meats, waiting at table and running errands. They learned to fish and hunt, to wrestle, fence and ride horseback. Seven years later the page became a squire, and his training became more rigorous. He had to practice a variety of military skills. Wearing full armor, he had to run, wrestle, scale a wall and wield a battle-ax—all without raising the visor of his helmet or catching a breath of fresh air.

At twenty-one the squire was ready to be knighted. The ceremony was long and elaborate. First there were religious duties to be performed—fasting, prayer and a priestly blessing of the knight's sword. Then, dressed in white garments, the young man knelt before his lord to pledge loyalty, piety and honor. Attendants dressed him in part of his armor, and he girded on his sword. Then he knelt once more before his lord to receive the accolade. This was the final part of the ceremony. The lord tapped the shoulder of the kneeling knight three times with the flat side of his sword. Then he spoke the words that completed the ritual. "In the name of God, of St. Michael, and St. George, I make thee a knight. Be valiant, courteous, and loyal." The new knight put on his helmet, shield and spear, and the ceremony was over.

Loyalty to his lord demanded that the knight be available for military action when called on. Courage in battle was even more important than skill. Opposing armies of knights on horseback charged directly at each other, and engaged in hand-to-hand combat. If a horse was wounded, his rider had small chance of defending himself. Therefore it was necessary to protect the animals too with armor.

The earliest armor was crudely shaped from leather. As men be-

213

came proficient in working metal, they fashioned protective garments of this new stronger material. Loops of metal were linked to other loops and sewn to leather or some other foundation to make chain mail. Steel plates were worn over the mail for additional protection. Later, knights went into battle in full armor—a complete outfit of solid metal, covering the knight from the top of his head down to his toes. Wealthy knights could afford elaborately decorated metal suits, and metalworkers outdid themselves, etching pictures and designs into the shiny, clanking garments they fashioned.

A complete metal outfit was a truly intricate piece of work. Each part was separate from the next, so that the wearer could move his joints. Greaves slipped over the feet to cover the legs below the knees. Cuisses covered the thighs, tied in back with strong leather thongs. Knee pieces covered the place where the greaves and cuisses met, and also tied in back. A corselet that covered the upper part of the body was made of chain mail; this garment was also known as a cuirass. On the knight's hands were gloves, or gauntlets, of mail. A doublet—a tunic or shirtlike garment—and a lined hood were worn under armor to protect the knight's body from being bruised by the metal.

Later, armor became more complicated. The helmet was made with several parts that moved—a visor, to protect the eyes, with slits to see through, and the gorget, or throat covering. Protective plates for the shoulders, chest, upper arms and hips were devised. A complete suit of armor might weigh as much as, or even more than, the man who wore it.

When a new kind of weapon, the gun, was invented, traditional armor became useless. In a gun battle a knight in full gear was handicapped. Soon this regalia was used only for ceremonial occasions, such as processions.

An armorer's workshop has been reconstructed at the Higgins Armory. The tools are similar to those later used by blacksmiths.

214

Armorer's workshop

There are an anvil, a vise, chisel, tongs and a variety of hammers. Some were used to flatten and spread the metal, making larger, thinner sheets.

Armorers also made strongboxes, elaborate locks and keys, and other decorative wrought-iron hardware. Many of these are in the Higgins collection. There are also stained-glass windows from churches and castles built during the age of knighthood.

In the gallery known as the Modern Wing are mass-produced iron and steel articles. Mixing bowls and airplane propellers can be handsomely designed and require skilled workmen too. One display shows how contemporary metal products are manufactured.

After your tour of the museum, you are welcome to watch craftsmen and machinists of the Worcester Pressed Steel factory at work.

215

31

MID-FAIRFIELD COUNTY
YOUTH MUSEUM
10 Woodside Lane (P.O. Box 165)
Westport, Connecticut 06880

BROOKLYN
CHILDREN'S MUSEUM
Brooklyn Avenue and Park Place
Brooklyn, New York 11213

CHILDREN'S MUSEUM
OF INDIANAPOLIS
3010 North Meridian Street
Indianapolis, Indiana 46208

FORT WORTH
CHILDREN'S MUSEUM
1501 Montgomery Street
Fort Worth, Texas 76107

THE CHILDREN'S MUSEUM
60 Burroughs Street
Boston, Massachusetts 02130

What kind of museum will invite you to climb down into a manhole and explore the pipes and cables beneath a city street? What kind of museum will sell you a mouse? Guide you on an archeological dig? Let you take care of its live animal exhibits? Ask you to hold an opossum in your lap while you listen to a lecture? Teach you to play games American Indians used to play?

A children's museum is that kind of place.

216

Exploring under city streets

Not all of them, of course, will allow you to do all these things. But every children's museum is a very special place. Its halls are small instead of vast and echoing. Within them, boys and girls are active participants, not just spectators.

The Mid-Fairfield County Youth Museum in Westport, Connecticut, was founded by John Ripley Forbes, who—as president of the Natural Science for Youth Foundation—has helped establish junior museums and young people's science centers all over the country. Mr. Forbes' special interest is live animal exhibits. In all the museums he has helped sponsor, young people can discover and begin to explore and understand the plant and animal life around them.

At Westport, foxes, snakes, raccoons, mice, salamanders, skunks and screech owls are part of the living menagerie. The museum stands on 53 acres of woods, fields and streams which are as important as the exhibits themselves. These grounds too are a place to discover nature's secrets. It surprised no one on the staff when a boy went off into the woods one night with a flashlight which he focused on a stream. He knew he would find spotted salamanders that had come there to lay their eggs.

As a tribute to the museum and the love of animals it encourages, the famous sculptress and friend of Mr. Forbes Anna Hyatt Huntington donated a bronze cast of one of her most delightful sculptures. Her statue of a bear with two cubs can be found just off the parking lot on the way to the front door. Children climb all over it. The most highly polished parts of the sculpture—highly polished from much handling—are the ears of the cubs and the top of the mother bear's head, which can be reached only by getting up onto her back.

In the museum, one of the exhibits visitors enjoy most is found in a darkened alcove with six portholes. Here you can pretend to be inside a bathysphere that is rising from the very bottom of the ocean to the surface, and look out at the different levels of underwater life as you come up. Special fluorescent lighting and realistic paintings produce ocean scenes that are biologically accurate and exciting. Another favorite display is a habitat group showing the invertebrates, birds and mammals found in the marshlands of this Connecticut community near Long Island Sound.

The Brooklyn Children's Museum, which opened its doors in 1899, was the first in the country or, indeed, in the world. It was established to "delight and instruct the children who visit it" and "to stimulate their power of observation and reflection." During all the years since it opened, its goal has been to interest young people in science as a career. Its unique facilities and special programs attract youngsters who already have a greater-than-average interest

Children examine objects from Indian collection.

in science. But its exhibits can be enjoyed by every visitor. The natural history displays include both living and mounted mammals, birds and reptiles. The cultural history department displays Indian artifacts, clothing from many parts of the world and a collection of antique dolls from many countries.

The Fort Worth Children's Museum is the largest in the world. It is housed in a handsome building that cost $2,500,000. It has a planetarium, a live animal room and a health museum. Geology, natural history and Texas history are among the subjects that can be explored here. Among the touch-and-feel exhibits are a ferocious-looking leopard and some not very friendly-looking bears.

An exhibit showing European men of 5,000 years ago performing brain surgery is one of the most popular. It is part of a group illustrating the history of medicine. The visitor is not separated from this display by glass. The figures of the men are on a slight mound built up from the floor. Only a railing keeps you from joining the group. You can feel almost as if you were back in prehistoric times, an actual observer of the real scene.

219

The Children's Museum of Indianapolis is not a nature center, but its exhibits cover a wide range of interest. Here you can see the mummy of an Egyptian princess, Wenuhotep. You can follow the history of travel from Indian trails to an Indianapolis Speedway racing car. You can visit an 1829 pioneer cabin reconstructed on the museum grounds and furnished just as it might have been when it was built. If you are lucky you may see a demonstration of broommaking, spinning, weaving, candle dipping, soapmaking, butter churning or muzzle loading. There is a Hall of Man which contains an Eskimo exhibit and an African collection. And there are natural history exhibits.

You will have to go to the Boston Children's Museum to get inside a manhole and crawl along under a city pavement. Before you get on your hands and knees, you are asked by the museum to try to find several things: a pipe through which gas comes into your home for your stove or furnace; a waterpipe hollowed out of a tree trunk by an early settler; old trolley car tracks; bundles of telephone wires going to houses and stores; and a storm sewer big enough to crawl into.

This is just one of museum director Michael Spock's unique exhibits called "What's Inside?" In others, you can investigate inside a greatly enlarged drop of water, a sewing machine, a Volkswagen engine, a telephone or an Indian grave. You can discover how a baby grows inside the mother's body. You can tear apart a flower and examine the parts under a microscope.

Who thinks these things up? The director and his staff. They spend hours just talking about ideas. And once an idea has been agreed upon, preparing the actual exhibit can take as much as twenty months.

There are now hundreds of children's museums around the country. No two are exactly alike. But the one thing they all have in common is that beyond their doors lies a special world created with *you* in mind.

APPENDIX

APPENDIX

OTHER HISTORY MUSEUMS FOR YOU TO VISIT

History and Development of Cities

Detroit Historical Museum, Detroit, Michigan

Atwater Kent Museum, Philadelphia, Pennsylvania

History and Development of States

Oregon Historical Society, Portland, Oregon

Ohio Historical Society, Columbus, Ohio

Museum Villages

Colonial Williamsburg, Williamsburg, Virginia
(English Colonial period)

Old Sturbridge Village, Old Sturbridge, Massachusetts
(New England just after the Revolution)

Plimoth Plantation, Plymouth, Massachusetts
(Reconstructed homes of Pilgrim Fathers)

Greenfield Village, Dearborn, Michigan
(Museum village created by Henry Ford to preserve scenes of his childhood and to honor his friend, Thomas Edison. Here is Edison's lab, where the incandescent lamp was invented; also the farmhouse where Ford was born)

Harold Warp Pioneer Village, Minden, Nebraska
(Tools and life of Midwest pioneers)

Richmondtown, Staten Island, New York
(Dutch Colonial era)

Sutter's Fort, California
(Stores, homes and warehouse of the 1849 gold rush community, with the fort where gold was found)

Fort Laramie, Wyoming
(A military base [1849–1890] and earlier fur-trading post)

Appendix

Industrial History

Crane Museum, Dalton, Massachusetts
(The story of papermaking from mill days to the present)
Merrimack Valley Textile Museum, North Andover, Massachusetts
(The history of wool manufacture stressing early 19th-century changes of
the Industrial Revolution)
Saugus Ironworks, Saugus, Massachusetts
(Early iron manufacture)
Early Iron Village of Batsto, Egg Harbor City, New Jersey
(Early iron manufacture)
Corning Glass Center Hall of Science and Industry, Corning, New York
(History of glassmaking)
Wells Fargo Bank History Room, San Francisco, California
(Bank history)
Eli Lilly and Company, Indianapolis, Indiana
(Drug manufacture from 1876 to present; original laboratory is re-created)

OTHER ART MUSEUMS FOR YOU TO VISIT

Among the Greatest in the World

Metropolitan Museum of Art, New York, New York
Museum of Fine Arts, Boston, Massachusetts
Art Institute of Chicago, Chicago, Illinois
Philadelphia Museum of Art, Philadelphia, Pennsylvania
Cleveland Museum of Art, Cleveland, Ohio
National Gallery of Art, Washington, D. C.

Oriental Art Can Be Found in:

Freer Gallery, Washington, D. C.
Los Angeles County Museum of Art, Los Angeles, California
Rhode Island School of Design, Providence, Rhode Island
(And the Museum of Fine Arts, Boston, and the Cleveland Museum of Art)

Fine Impressionist Collections Are at:

Art Institute of Chicago
Philadelphia Museum of Art
Cleveland Museum of Art
National Gallery of Art

224

Contemporary American and European Art Can Be Seen at:

Carnegie Institute, Museum of Art, Pittsburgh, Pennsylvania
Albright-Knox Gallery, Buffalo, New York
Munson-Williams Proctor Institute, Utica, New York
Solomon Guggenheim Museum of Art, New York, New York
Museum of Modern Art, New York, New York
Roswell Museum and Art Center, Roswell, New Mexico
"Old Hundred," Ridgefield, Connecticut

OTHER SCIENCE MUSEUMS FOR YOU TO VISIT

Physical and Natural Sciences

California Academy of Sciences Museum, San Francisco, California
Franklin Institute, Philadelphia, Pennsylvania
Museum of Science, Boston, Massachusetts
Oregon Museum of Science and Industry, Portland, Oregon
Museum of Science and Industry, Chicago, Illinois
Rochester Museum of Arts and Sciences, Rochester, New York
Museum of History and Technology of Smithsonian Institution, Washington, D. C.

Planetariums

Hayden Planetarium of the American Museum of Natural History, New York, New York
Griffith Observatory and Planetarium, Los Angeles, California
Buhl Planetarium and Institute of Popular Science, Pittsburgh, Pennsylvania
Fels Planetarium of Franklin Institute, Philadelphia, Pennsylvania

Natural Sciences

American Museum of Natural History, New York, New York
Museum of Natural History, Chicago, Illinois
Museum of Natural History of the Smithsonian Institution, Washington, D. C.

Zoos

Bronx Zoo, New York, New York
National Zoological Park, Washington, D. C.

Chicago Zoo, Chicago, Illinois
Philadelphia Zoo, Philadelphia, Pennsylvania

Health Museums

Dallas Health and Science Museum, Dallas, Texas
Hinsdale Health Museum, Hinsdale, Illinois

MORE VERY SPECIAL PLACES

General Museums

Los Angeles County Museum of History and Science, Los Angeles, California
Oakland Museum, Oakland, California
(Combines art, natural history, local anthropology and local history)
Reading Public Museum and Art Gallery, Reading, Pennsylvania
(Combines art, natural history and a botanical garden)

Wild West Museums

Amon Carter Museum of Western Art, Fort Worth, Texas
(Indian art and artifacts and art of the West)
Thomas Gilcrease Institute of American History and Art, Tulsa, Oklahoma
(Indian art and artifacts and art of the West)
National Cowboy Hall of Fame and Western Heritage Center, Oklahoma City, Oklahoma
(A romantic view of traditional Western hero)

SELECTED LIST OF MUSEUMS IN THE UNITED STATES

There are more than 4,500 museums in the country. Only a fraction of them can be listed here. For a more complete descriptive listing, see the Appendix to *Museums, U.S.A., a History and Guide* by the authors of this book. The American Association of Museums publishes a comprehensive *Museums Directory of the United States and Canada,* useful for names and addresses, which can be consulted at many reference libraries. And a list of art museums can be found in the *American Art Directory,* published by the American Federation of Arts.

There are about 200 children's or junior museums in the country, and new ones open every year. Also there are several hundred nature centers and school nature museums which offer special activities for young people. The most up-to-date list of children's museums and nature centers can be obtained from the Natural Science for Youth Foundation, 114 East 30th Street, New York, New York 10016.

The listing which follows is arranged alphabetically, by state and by city. The name and address and a brief indication of the types of collections are given. When planning a museum trip, check visiting hours in advance. Because these are subject to change, they were not included here. Most museums charge either nothing, or very nominal admission fees. Since these, too, are subject to change, they are not included here.

ALABAMA

Birmingham Museum of Art
200 Eighth Avenue, N., Birmingham, Alabama

Tuskegee Institute, George Washington Carver Museum; Negro history and American and African art
PO Box 40, Tuskegee, Alabama

ALASKA

University of Alaska Museum; natural history
College, Alaska

Alaska Historical Library and Museum; state history, Indians
PO Box 2051, Juneau, Alaska

ARIZONA

The Heard Museum of Anthropology and Primitive Art
22 E. Monte Vista Road, Phoenix, Arizona

Phoenix Art Museum
1625 N. Central Avenue, Phoenix, Arizona

Arizona-Sonora Desert Museum
Tucson Mountain Park (PO Box 5602), Tucson, Arizona

University of Arizona, Arizona State Museum; anthropology, Indians
North Park Avenue at Third Street, Tucson, Arizona

Appendix

University of Arizona Art Gallery
Olive Road and Speedway, Tucson, Arizona

ARKANSAS

The Arkansas Art Center
MacArthur Park, Little Rock, Arkansas

CALIFORNIA

California Museum of Science and Industry
700 State Drive, Los Angeles, California

Griffith Observatory and Planetarium
Griffith Park (PO Box 27787, Los Feliz Station), Los Angeles, California

Griffith Park Zoo
4730 Crystal Springs Drive, Los Angeles, California

Los Angeles County Museum of Art
5905 Wilshire Boulevard, Los Angeles, California

Los Angeles County Museum of History and Science
900 Exposition Boulevard, Exposition Park, Los Angeles, California

Oakland Museum; art, local history, Indians, natural history
Civic Center between 10th and 12th Streets, Oakland, California

Palm Springs Desert Museum; natural history, art, botanical garden
135 East Tahquitz Drive, Palm Springs, California

E. B. Crocker Art Gallery
216 O Street, Sacramento, California

Sutter's Fort State Historical Monument; historic house, gold rush period
2701 L Street, Sacramento, California

San Diego Natural History Museum
Balboa Park (PO Box 1390), San Diego, California

San Diego Zoological Garden
Balboa Park (PO Box 551), San Diego, California

California Academy of Sciences, Morrison Planetarium,
Science Museum, Steinhart Aquarium
Golden Gate Park, San Francisco, California

California Palace of the Legion of Honor; art
Lincoln Park, San Francisco, California

M. H. de Young Memorial Museum; art
Golden Gate Park, San Francisco, California

San Francisco Museum of Art
McAllister Street at Van Ness Avenue, San Francisco, California

Wells Fargo Bank History Room; history of Wells, Fargo Company, gold rush
and early city history
420 Montgomery Street, San Francisco, California

Henry E. Huntington Library and Art Gallery; art, rare books, botanical garden
1151 Oxford Road, San Marino, California

COLORADO

Central Gold Mine and Museum; historic building, old gold mine
Central City, Colorado

Colorado Springs Fine Arts Center and Taylor Museum; art
30 W. Dale Street, Colorado Springs, Colorado

228

Colorado State Museum; state history
E. 14th Avenue and Sherman Street, Denver, Colorado

Denver Art Museum
W. 14th Avenue at Acoma Street, Denver, Colorado

Denver Museum of Natural History
City Park, Denver, Colorado

Colorado Railroad Museum; transportation history, in town where transcontinental railroad was completed
17155 W. 44th Avenue Road (PO Box 641), Golden, Colorado

CONNECTICUT

The Bruce Museum; natural history, live animals, art, Indians
Bruce Park, Greenwich, Connecticut

The Children's Museum of Hartford
950 Trout Brook Drive, Hartford, Connecticut

Wadsworth Atheneum; art
25 Atheneum Square, Hartford, Connecticut

Mystic Seaport Marine Historical Association; preservation project: New England port and village, ships and maritime equipment
Greenville Avenue, Mystic, Connecticut

Yale University Peabody Museum of Natural History
170 Whitney Avenue, New Haven, Connecticut

"Old Hundred"; contemporary art in historic house
Main Street, Ridgefield, Connecticut

The Stamford Museum and Nature Center; natural history, live animals
High Ridge at Scofieldtown Road, Stamford, Connecticut

The Mid-Fairfield County Youth Museum
10 Woodside Lane, Westport, Connecticut

DELAWARE

The Delaware State Museum; state history, historic house
316 S. Governors Avenue, Dover, Delaware

Hagley Museum; history of Du Pont Company and mill industry
Greenville, Wilmington, Delaware

The Henry Francis Du Pont Winterthur Museum; American art and furnishings, historic house, botanical garden
Winterthur, Delaware

DISTRICT OF COLUMBIA

Dumbarton Oaks Collection; pre-Columbian and Byzantine art, historic house, botanical garden
1703 32d Street, N. W., Washington, D.C.

Freer Gallery
12th and Jefferson Dr., S.W., Washington, D.C.

Lincoln Museum; Ford's Theater, where Lincoln was shot
511 10th Street, N.W., Washington, D.C.

National Gallery of Art
Constitution Avenue at Sixth Street, Washington, D.C.

National Geographic Society, Explorer's Hall; history of explorations
17th and M Streets, N.W., Washington, D.C.

Appendix

The Phillips Collection; art
1600–1612 21st Street, N.W., Washington, D.C.

Smithsonian Institution, Freer Gallery of Art; Oriental art
Jefferson Drive at 12th Street, S.W., On the Mall, Washington, D.C.

Smithsonian Institution, Museum of History and Technology; national history, physical science, industrial science
Constitution Avenue at 14th Street, N.W., On the Mall, Washington, D.C.

Smithsonian Institution, Museum of Natural History
Constitution Avenue at 10th Street, N.W., On the Mall, Washington, D.C.

Smithsonian Institution, National Air Museum; air and space transportation
Ninth Street and Jefferson Drive, S.W., On the Mall, Washington, D.C.

Smithsonian Institution, National Collection of Fine Arts and National Portrait Gallery; American art, portraits of famous Americans, historic house—Old Patent Office Building of 1837
Ninth and F Streets, N.W., Washington, D.C.

Smithsonian Institution, National Zoological Park
3000 Connecticut Avenue, N.W., Washington, D.C.

FLORIDA

University of Miami, Joe and Emily Lowe Art Gallery
1301 Miller Road, Coral Gables, Florida

University of Florida, Florida State Museum; natural history, archaeology and anthropology
Gainesville, Florida

Museum of Science and Natural History and Space Transit Planetarium
3280 S. Miami Avenue, Miami, Florida

Vizcaya: Dade County Art Museum; historic house, fine furnishings
3251 S. Miami Avenue, Miami, Florida

Castillo de San Marcos National Monument; historic fort and building
1 Castillo Drive, St. Augustine, Florida

The John and Mable Ringling Museum of Art, Ringling Residence, and Ringling Museum of the Circus
5401 Bay Shore Road, Sarasota, Florida

Norton Gallery and School of Art
Pioneer Park, West Palm Beach, Florida

GEORGIA

Atlanta Art Association; art museum
1280 Peachtree Street, N.E., Atlanta, Georgia

HAWAII

Bernice P. Bishop Museum; natural history
1355 Kalihi Street, Honolulu, Hawaii

Honolulu Academy of Arts
900 S. Beretania Street, Honolulu, Hawaii

Ulu Mau Village; preservation project: native Hawaiian village
Ala Moana Park (PO Box 3781), Honolulu, Hawaii

IDAHO

Idaho Historical Society; state and regional history
610 N. Julia Davis Drive, Boise, Idaho

ILLINOIS

Adler Planetarium and Astronomical Museum
900 E. Achsah Bond Drive, Chicago, Illinois

The Art Institute of Chicago
Michigan Avenue at Adams Street, Chicago, Illinois

Chicago Historical Society; local history, Civil War and Lincolniana
North Avenue and Clark Street, Chicago, Illinois

Chicago Natural History Museum
Roosevelt Road and Lake Shore Drive, Chicago, Illinois

Lincoln Park Zoological Garden
100 W. Webster Avenue, Chicago, Illinois

Museum of Science and Industry
57th and S. Lake Shore Drive, Chicago, Illinois

Hinsdale Health Museum
40 S. Clay Street, Hinsdale, Illinois

Illinois State Museum of Natural History and Art
Spring and Edwards Streets, Springfield, Illinois

INDIANA

John Herron Museum of Art
110 E. 16th Street, Indianapolis, Indiana

Children's Museum of Indianapolis
3010 N. Meridian Street, Indianapolis, Indiana

Eli Lilly and Company Museum; company museum, pharmaceutical industry
645 S. Alabama Street, Indianapolis, Indiana

University of Notre Dame Art Gallery
O'Shaughnessy Hall of Liberal and Fine Arts, Notre Dame, Indiana

IOWA

Davenport Public Museum; natural history, local history, art
1717 W. 12th Street, Davenport, Iowa

Des Moines Art Center
Greenwood Park, Des Moines, Iowa

Iowa State Museum; natural history, space science, state history
State Department of History and Archives,
E. 12th and Grand Avenue, Des Moines, Iowa

KANSAS

Old Shawnee Mission; historic buildings, early state history
3403 W. 53d Street, Kansas City, Kansas

Kansas State Historical Society Museum
Memorial Building, 120 W. 10th Street, Topeka, Kansas

Wichita Art Museum
619 Stackman Drive, Wichita, Kansas

KENTUCKY

J. B. Speed Art Museum
2035 S. Third Street, Louisville, Kentucky

231

Appendix

LOUISIANA

Isaac Delgado Museum of Art
Lelong Avenue, City Park, New Orleans, Louisiana

New Orleans Jazz Museum; popular music, Negro influence in music
1017 Dumaine Street, New Orleans, Louisiana

MAINE

Portland Museum of Art; American art, historic house
111 High Street, Portland, Maine

The Wadsworth-Longfellow House; historic house, state history
Maine Historical Society, 485–487 Congress Street, Portland, Maine

William A. Farnsworth Library and Art Museum
19 Elm Street, Rockland, Maine

Penobscot Marine Museum; maritime history, historic buildings
Church Street, Searsport, Maine

Old Gaol Museum; local history, old jail of 1653
Route 1A, York, Maine

MARYLAND

Baltimore and Ohio Transportation Museum; railroad history
Pratt and Poppleton Streets, Baltimore, Maryland

The Baltimore Museum of Art
Wyman Park, Baltimore, Maryland

Fort McHenry National Monument
Baltimore, Maryland

Maryland Historical Society
210 W. Monument Street, Baltimore, Maryland

The Peale Museum; local history, American art
225 N. Holliday Street, Baltimore, Maryland

The Walters Art Gallery; classical, Byzantine, medieval, Renaissance art and
   decorative arts
Charles and Centre Streets, Baltimore, Maryland

MASSACHUSETTS

The Children's Museum
60 Burroughs Street, Boston, Massachusetts

Isabella Stewart Gardner Museum; art
280 The Fenway, Boston, Massachusetts

Museum of Fine Arts
469 Huntington Avenue, Boston, Massachusetts

Museum of Science; natural and physical sciences
Science Park, Boston, Massachusetts

Crane Museum; company museum, papermaking industry
South Street, Dalton, Massachusetts

Indian House Memorial; local history, folk art, historic house
Main Street, Deerfield, Massachusetts

Pocumtuck Valley Memorial Association; local history, historic building
Deerfield, Massachusetts

Nantucket Historical Association; historic houses, local history, whaling
Fair Street, Nantucket, Massachusetts

232

Old Dartmouth Historical Society Whaling Museum
18 Johnny Cake Hill, New Bedford, Massachusetts

Merrimack Valley Textile Museum; history of wool manufacture
Massachusetts Avenue, North Andover, Massachusetts

Pilgrim Hall; local history
Court Street, Plymouth, Massachusetts

Plimoth Plantation, Inc.; replica of Pilgrim village
Warren Avenue (PO Box 1620), Plymouth, Massachusetts

Essex Institute; local history, historic houses
132 Essex Street, Salem, Massachusetts

Peabody Museum of Salem; local natural history, maritime history, ethnology of
the Pacific
161 Essex Street, Salem, Massachusetts

Saugus Ironworks Restoration; early iron works, historic buildings, seventeenth
century
244 Central Street (PO Box 1127), Saugus, Massachusetts

Springfield Science Museum; natural history, planetarium
236 State Street, Springfield, Massachusetts

Old Sturbridge Village; historic buildings: New England village of 1790–1840
Sturbridge, Massachusetts

Sterling and Francine Clark Art Institute
South Street, Williamstown, Massachusetts

Williams College Museum of Art
Main Street, Williamstown, Massachusetts

The John Woodman Higgins Armory
100 Barber Avenue, Worcester, Massachusetts

Worcester Art Museum
55 Salisbury Street, Worcester, Massachusetts

Worcester Science Museums; natural history
21 Cedar Street and 41 Elm Street, Worcester, Massachusetts

MICHIGAN

Cranbrook Institute of Science; physical science, natural history
500 Lone Pine Road, Bloomfield Hills, Michigan

Henry Ford Museum and Greenfield Village; historic buildings, history of
transportation, industry, early American village
Dearborn, Michigan

Children's Museum, Detroit Public Schools
67 E. Kirby Avenue, Detroit, Michigan

Detroit Historical Museum; local history, historic buildings
5401 Woodward Avenue, Detroit, Michigan

Detroit Institute of Arts
5200 Woodward Avenue, Detroit, Michigan

Money Museum, National Bank of Detroit; numismatics
Fort and Woodward Streets, Detroit, Michigan

Grand Rapids Public Museum; local history, natural history
54 Jefferson Avenue, S.E., Grand Rapids, Michigan

Mackinac Island State Park Commission and Fort Michilimackinac; historic
buildings, site of first battle of War of 1812
PO Box 523, Mackinac Island, Michigan

233

Appendix

MINNESOTA

A. M. Chisholm Museum; children's museum
1832 E. Second Street, Duluth, Minnesota

Minneapolis Institute of Arts
201 E. 34th Street, Minneapolis, Minnesota

Walker Art Center
1710 Lyndale Avenue S., Minneapolis, Minnesota

Mayo Medical Museum
Third Avenue and First Street, S.W., Rochester, Minnesota

MISSISSIPPI

Natchez Trace Parkway; historic house, old Indian trails and post road
PO Box 948, Tupelo, Mississippi

MISSOURI

William Rockhill Nelson Gallery and Atkins Museum of Fine Arts
4525 Oak Street, Kansas City, Missouri

City Art Museum of St. Louis
Forest Park, St. Louis, Missouri

Missouri Botanical Garden
2315 Tower Grove Avenue, St. Louis, Missouri

National Museum of Transport; all forms of transportation
3022 Barretts Station Road, St. Louis, Missouri

MONTANA

Museum of the Plains Indian
Browning, Montana

Montana Historical Society; state history, art of the West
Roberts at Fifth Avenue, Helena, Montana

NEBRASKA

Nebraska State Historical Society Museum
1500 R Street, Lincoln, Nebraska

Sheldon Memorial Art Gallery, University of Nebraska
12th and R Streets, Lincoln, Nebraska

The Harold Warp Pioneer Village; reconstruction of old village
Highway 6, 34, 10, Minden, Nebraska

Joslyn Art Museum
2218 Dodge Street, Omaha, Nebraska

NEVADA

Nevada State Museum; state history, natural history
N. Carson Street, Carson City, Nevada

NEW HAMPSHIRE

The Currier Gallery of Art
192 Orange Street, Manchester, New Hampshire

The O. Rundle Gilbert Museum of Original U.S. Patent Models
Route 3, Plymouth, New Hampshire

Strawberry Banke; restoration of historic buildings
Portsmouth, New Hampshire

NEW JERSEY

Early Iron Village of Batsto; historic buildings, old ironworks
Wharton Tract Office, RD 2, Egg Harbor City, New Jersey

U.S. Army Signal Corps Museum; history of military communications
Myer Hall, Avenue of Memories, Fort Monmouth, New Jersey

The Newark Museum; art, science, local history
43–49 Washington Street, Newark, New Jersey

New Jersey State Museum; history, science, anthropology
State Cultural Center, Trenton, New Jersey

Edison National Historic Site; home and laboratories of Thomas A. Edison
Main Street at Lakeside Avenue, West Orange, New Jersey

NEW MEXICO

Roswell Museum and Art Center; art, natural history, space science and rocketry
11th and Main Streets, Roswell, New Mexico

Museum of Navajo Ceremonial Art
Camino Lejo, off Old Pecos Road, Santa Fe, New Mexico

Museum of New Mexico; Fine Arts Museum
127 E. Palace Avenue (PO Box 1727), Santa Fe, New Mexico

Museum of New Mexico, Hall of Ethnology; regional anthropology and archaeology, Southwest Indians
Lincoln Avenue (PO Box 1727), Santa Fe, New Mexico

Museum of New Mexico, Museum of International Folk Art
Old Pecos Trail (Camino Lejo), PO Box 1727, Sante Fe, New Mexico

Museum of New Mexico; Palace of the Governors; historic building, 1610, and
state history
Palace Avenue (PO Box 1727), Santa Fe, New Mexico

NEW YORK

Albany Institute of History and Art;
125 Washington Avenue, Albany, New York

New York State Museum and Science Service; natural history
31 Washington Avenue, Albany, New York

Adirondack Museum; local history, lumbering
Blue Mountain Lake, New York

The Buffalo Fine Arts Academy, Albright-Knox Art Gallery
1285 Elmwood Avenue, Buffalo, New York

Buffalo Museum of Science; natural history
Humboldt Park, Buffalo, New York

Whaling Museum
Main Street, Cold Spring Harbor, Long Island, New York

Cooperstown Indian Museum
1 Pioneer Street (PO Box 123), Cooperstown, New York

National Baseball Hall of Fame and Museum
Main Street, Cooperstown, New York

*New York State Historical Association; Farmer's Museum, Village Crossroads,
Fenimore House;* historic buildings, folk art
Lake Road, Cooperstown, New York

The Woodland Museum; local natural history
Lake Road, Cooperstown, New York

235

Appendix

Corning Glass Center, Hall of Science and Industry and Corning Museum of Glass; company museum: history of glass industry
Houghton Park, Corning, New York

Old Museum Village of Smith's Cove; historic buildings, nineteenth-century town
Monroe, New York

The American Museum of Natural History and Hayden Planetarium
Central Park West at 79th Street, New York, New York

The American Numismatic Society
Broadway between 155th and 156th Streets, New York, New York

Brooklyn Botanic Garden
1000 Washington Avenue, Brooklyn, New York

Brooklyn Children's Museum
Brooklyn Avenue and Park Place, Brooklyn, New York

Brooklyn Museum; art
188 Eastern Parkway, Brooklyn, New York

The Chase Manhattan Bank Money Museum
50th Street at Avenue of the Americas, New York, New York

The Metropolitan Museum of Art
Fifth Avenue at 82d Street, New York, New York

The Metropolitan Museum of Art, The Cloisters
Fort Tryon Park, New York, New York

Museum of the American Indian
Broadway at 155th Street, New York, New York

Museum of the City of New York; local history
1220 Fifth Avenue, New York, New York

Museum of Contemporary Crafts; work by today's craftsmen
29 W. 53d Street, New York, New York

Museum of Early American Folk Arts
49 W. 53d Street, New York, New York

Museum of Modern Art
11 W. 53d Street, New York, New York

Museum of Primitive Art; art of Africa, Oceania, pre-Columbian America, etc.
15 W. 54th Street, New York, New York

The New York Aquarium
Boardwalk at W. Eighth Street, Coney Island, Brooklyn, New York

The New York Botanical Garden
Bronx Park, Bedford Park Boulevard, New York, New York
The New-York Historical Society; city and state history
170 Central Park West, New York, New York

The New York Zoological Park (The Bronx Zoo)
Bronx Park, Fordham Road and Pelham Parkway, New York, New York

The Solomon R. Guggenheim Museum; modern art, building designed by Frank Lloyd Wright
1071 Fifth Avenue, New York, New York

Staten Island Historical Society, Richmondtown Restoration; Dutch-English colonial village
Court Place and Center Street, Staten Island, New York

Whitney Museum of American Art
945 Madison Avenue, New York, New York

Washington's Headquarters and Museum; historic house of 1750, Revolutionary War
84 Liberty Street, Newburgh, New York

The Shaker Museum; buildings, furnishings, crafts of the Shaker religious community
Shaker Museum Road, Old Chatham, New York

George Eastman House; history of photography, as science, art and industry
900 East Avenue, Rochester, New York

Rochester Museum of Arts and Sciences; natural history, local history
657 East Avenue, Rochester, New York

Canal Museum; Erie Canal history, building
Erie Boulevard E., Syracuse, New York

Munson-Williams-Proctor Institute; art museum
310 Genesee Street, Utica, New York

West Point Museum; United States Military Academy
West Point, New York

NORTH CAROLINA

University of North Carolina, The Morehead Planetarium
Chapel Hill, North Carolina

Charlotte Children's Nature Museum
1658 Sterling Road, Charlotte, North Carolina

North Carolina Museum of Art
107 E. Morgan Street, Raleigh, North Carolina

Old Salem; historic buildings, furnishings
600 S. Main Street, Salem, North Carolina

NORTH DAKOTA

Theodore Roosevelt National Memorial Park Visitor Center; Maltese Cross Ranch of T. Roosevelt; natural history
Medora, North Dakota

OHIO

Cincinnati Art Museum
Eden Park, Cincinnati, Ohio

The Taft Museum; art, decorative arts, historic house, 1820
316 Pike Street, Cincinnati, Ohio

Cleveland Health Museum
8911 Euclid Avenue, Cleveland, Ohio

The Cleveland Museum of Art
11150 East Boulevard, Cleveland, Ohio

Natural Science Museum
10600 East Boulevard, Cleveland, Ohio

The Western Reserve Historical Society; state history, early aircraft and automobiles
10825 East Boulevard, Cleveland, Ohio

The Columbus Gallery of Fine Arts
480 Broad Street, Columbus, Ohio

The Museum of the Ohio Historical Society; state history, historic sites and buildings throughout Ohio, archaeology
1813 N. High Street, Columbus, Ohio

Appendix

Air Force Museum; history of military aviation
Wright-Patterson Air Force Base, Dayton, Ohio

Dayton Art Institute
405 W. Riverview Avenue, Dayton, Ohio

Dayton Museum of Natural History
2629 Ridge Avenue, Dayton, Ohio

Toledo Museum of Art
Monroe Street and Scottwood Avenue, Toledo, Ohio

Butler Institute of American Art
524 Wick Avenue, Youngstown, Ohio

OKLAHOMA

Indian City, U.S.A.; re-creation of Plains Indian villages
PO Box 356, Anadarko, Oklahoma

U.S. Army Artillery and Missile Center Museum
346 Randolph Road, Fort Sill, Oklahoma

National Cowboy Hall of Fame and Western Heritage Center; the old West
N.E. Expressway and Eastern, Oklahoma City, Oklahoma

Philbrook Art Center
2727 S. Rockford Road, Tulsa, Oklahoma

The Thomas Gilcrease Institute of American History and Art; art, Indians of the
Plains
2401 W. Newton Street, Tulsa, Oklahoma

OREGON

Oregon Historical Society
Public Auditorium, 235 S.W. Market Street, Portland, Oregon

Oregon Museum of Science and Industry; natural and physical sciences
4015 S.W. Canyon Road, Portland, Oregon

Portland Art Museum
S.W. Park and Madison Streets, Portland, Oregon

PENNSYLVANIA

Allentown Art Museum
Fifth and Court Streets, Allentown, Pennsylvania

Old Economy; historic houses of nineteenth-century utopian community
14th and Church Streets, Ambridge, Pennsylvania

Cornwall Furnace; historic buildings, early ironmaking industry
PO Box V, Cornwall, Pennsylvania

Mercer Museum of the Bucks County Historical Society; local and farm history,
early handicrafts
Pine and Ashland Streets, Doylestown, Pennsylvania

Gettysburg National Military Park Visitor Center; Civil War battleground and
buildings
Gettysburg, Pennsylvania

William Penn Memorial Museum; state history, natural history
Harrisburg, Pennsylvania

Pennsylvania Farm Museum of Landis Valley; historic buildings, Pennsylvania
Dutch, handcrafts
2451 Kissel Hill Road, Lancaster, Pennsylvania

238

The Academy of Natural Sciences of Philadelphia
19th Street and The Parkway, Philadelphia, Pennsylvania

Atwater Kent Museum; city history
15 S. Seventh Street, Philadelphia, Pennsylvania

The Franklin Institute and Fels Planetarium; physical sciences and industry
20th Street and The Parkway, Philadelphia, Pennsylvania

Independence National Historical Park; Independence Hall and other buildings
   of Revolutionary and early Federal period
420 Chestnut Street, Philadelphia, Pennsylvania

Philadelphia Museum of Art
Benjamin Franklin Parkway at 26th Street, Philadelphia, Pennsylvania

Commercial Museum; ethnography, industry, city planning
34th Street and Convention Avenue, Philadelphia, Pennsylvania

University Museum, University of Pennsylvania; anthropology and archaeology
33d and Spruce Streets, Philadelphia, Pennsylvania

Zoological Society of Philadelphia
34th Street and Girard Avenue, Philadelphia, Pennsylvania

Buhl Planetarium and Institute of Popular Science
Federal and Ohio Streets, Pittsburgh, Pennsylvania

Carnegie Institute, Carnegie Museum; natural history
4400 Forbes Avenue, Pittsburgh, Pennsylvania

Carnegie Institute, Museum of Art
4400 Forbes Avenue, Pittsburgh, Pennsylvania

The Reading Public Museum and Art Gallery; art, botanical garden, natural
   history
500 Museum Road, Reading, Pennsylvania

RHODE ISLAND

Newport Historical Society; state and local history, decorative arts, historic
   houses
82 Touro Street, Newport, Rhode Island

Rhode Island School of Design Museum of Art
224 Benefit Street, Providence, Rhode Island

SOUTH CAROLINA

The Charleston Museum; local history and natural history, first museum in the
   United States
125 Rutledge Avenue, Charleston, South Carolina

Columbia Museum of Art and Science
Senate and Bull Streets, Columbia, South Carolina

SOUTH DAKOTA

Sioux Indian Museum
1002 St. Joseph Street, Rapid City, South Dakota

TENNESSEE

Brooks Memorial Art Gallery
Overton Park, Memphis, Tennessee

Children's Museum
724 Second Avenue S., Nashville, Tennessee

239

Appendix

American Museum of Atomic Energy
Jefferson Circle (PO Box 117), Oak Ridge, Tennessee

TEXAS

Corpus Christi Museum; natural history, local history, children's museum
1202 N. Water Street, Corpus Christi, Texas

Dallas Health and Science Museum
Fair Park, Dallas, Texas

Dallas Museum of Fine Arts
Fair Park, Dallas, Texas

El Paso Museum of Art
1211 Montana Avenue, El Paso, Texas

Amon Carter Museum of Western Art; American and regional art
3501 Camp Bowie Boulevard, Fort Worth, Texas

Fort Worth Art Center
1309 Montgomery Street, Fort Worth, Texas

Fort Worth Children's Museum
1501 Montgomery Street, Fort Worth, Texas

Museum of Fine Arts of Houston
1001 Bissonnet, Houston, Texas

The Alamo; state history
San Antonio, Texas

Witte Memorial Museum; natural history, regional history and historic houses,
   regional art
3801 Broadway, San Antonio, Texas

UTAH

Dinosaur National Monument Visitor Center; dinosaur bones can be seen in
   place in the earth
(Mail: Box 101, Artesia, Colorado), Jensen, Utah

Latter-Day Saints Museum, Lion House; history of Mormon settlers, historic
   house of Brigham Young
Temple Square, Salt Lake City, Utah

Pioneer Village Museum; historic buildings
2998 Connor Street, Salt Lake City, Utah

Utah Field Museum of Natural History; state archeology and natural history
Vernal State Park, Main Street, Vernal, Utah

VERMONT

The Bennington Museum; local history, industry, art
W. Main Street, Bennington, Vermont

Shelburne Museum; folk arts, historic houses
Shelburne Road, Shelburne, Vermont

VIRGINIA

Appomattox Court House National Historical Park; restored village of 1865
Appomattox, Virginia

Jamestown Foundation; reconstructed site of first English settlement in America
Jamestown, Virginia

The Mariners Museum
Museum Drive, Newport News, Virginia

240

Confederate Museum, White House of the Confederacy; historic house, Civil War
1201 Clay Street, Richmond, Virginia

Virginia Museum of Fine Arts
Boulevard and Grove Avenue, Richmond, Virginia

Abby Aldrich Rockefeller Folk Art Collection
Colonial Williamsburg, Williamsburg, Virginia

Colonial Williamsburg; historic buildings: Colonial town, about 450 buildings
including houses, shops; decorative arts, crafts
Williamsburg, Virginia

WASHINGTON

Museum of History and Industry; local and industrial history
2161 E. Hamlin Street, Seattle, Washington

Pacific Science Center; physical science, natural history, space science, children's
science laboratory, live animals
200 Second Avenue N., Seattle, Washington

Seattle Art Museum
Volunteer Park, Seattle, Washington

WEST VIRGINIA

The Children's Museum and Planetarium of Charleston
"Sunrise," 746 Myrtle Road, Charleston, West Virginia

WISCONSIN

Museum of the State Historical Society of Wisconsin; and historic sites throughout state
816 State Street, Madison, Wisconsin

Milwaukee Art Center
Milwaukee County War Memorial Building, 750 N. Lincoln Memorial Drive,
Milwaukee, Wisconsin

Milwaukee Public Museum; natural history, anthropology
800 W. Wells Street, Milwaukee, Wisconsin

WYOMING

Wyoming State Museum; state and regional history
State Office Building, 23d and Central Avenues, Cheyenne, Wyoming

Buffalo Bill Museum; Wild West history
Buffalo Bill Historical Center, 836 Sheridan Avenue (PO Box 1262), Cody,
Wyoming

Whitney Gallery of Western Art
Buffalo Bill Historical Center, 720 Sheridan Avenue (PO Box 1020), Cody,
Wyoming

PUERTO RICO

El Museo de Arte de Ponce; art, botanical garden
Ponce, Puerto Rico

San Juan National Historic Site; history of the island, historic buildings
Norzagany Street (PO Box 712), San Juan, Puerto Rico

PHOTO ACKNOWLEDGMENTS

Credit for the photographic illustrations in this book is gratefully acknowledged to the following:

The Peale Museum, Baltimore, pages 16, 17
Pennsylvania Farm Museum of Landis Valley, pages 21, 22, 23
The Byron Collection, Museum of the City of New York, page 26
Museum of the City of New York, page 27
Shelburne Museum, Inc., pages 31, 33, 34, 37, 38
Nebraska State Historical Society, pages 41, 42
State Historical Society of Wisconsin, photo by Paul Vanderbilt, page 25
State Historical Society of Wisconsin, pages 47, 49
Hagley Museum, pages 53, 54, 56, 57, 58
Kansas City *Star,* page 62
William Rockhill Nelson Gallery of Art and the Atkins Museum of Fine Arts, pages 63, 66
Whitney Museum of American Art, New York, pages 68, 70, 71
Whitney Museum of American Art, photo by Ezra Stoller, page 72
The Phillips Collection, Washington, D.C., pages 74, 75, 76
The Brooklyn Museum, pages 79, 81, 82, 83, 84
Baltimore Museum of Art, page 89
Library of Congress collection, page 90
The Toledo Museum of Art, pages 92, 93, 94, 95
Seattle Art Museum, pages 98, 99, 101
Wadsworth Atheneum, Hartford, Connecticut, pages 104, 106, 107, 108
Ringling Museum of Art, page 110
Ringling Museum of the Circus, pages 112, 113, 114
The Detroit Institute of the Arts, pages 116, 120
Cranbrook Institute of Science, page 125
Cranbrook Academy of Art, page 127
Adler Planetarium, page 135
National Aeronautics and Space Administration, page 136
Denver Museum of Natural History, page 141
Arizona-Sonora Desert Museum, photo by Mervin W. Larson, page 146
Arizona-Sonora Desert Museum, page 150
Museum of the American Indian, Heye Foundation, pages 152, 154, 156
San Diego Zoo, Ron Garrison, pages 158, 159
Missouri Botanical Garden, photo by Claude Johnston, pages 165, 167
Cleveland Health Museum, page 171
The Newark Museum, Newark, New Jersey, pages 176, 179, 181, 182, 183, 184
New York State Historical Association, Cooperstown, New York, pages 188, 189, 191
Baseball Hall of Fame, Cooperstown, New York, Vincent Civiletti painting, page 192
Whitney Gallery of Western Art, pages 195, 199
The Mariners Museum, Newport News, Virginia, pages 201, 203, 205
Baltimore and Ohio Transportation Museum, page 207
The John Woodman Higgins Armory, pages 212, 215
Westport Children's Museum, page 217
Brooklyn Children's Museum, page 219

INDEX

INDEX

Figures in italics refer to illustrations on those pages.

245

Index

ABOUT THE AUTHORS

HERBERT and MARJORIE KATZ are both native New Yorkers. Mr. Katz's field is English literature, and Mrs. Katz's field is anthropology.

Combining their interests, they collaborated as authors on a book called *Museums, U.S.A.—A History and Guide,* published by Doubleday in 1965. This led to several magazine articles. MUSEUM ADVENTURES marks their second collaborative effort. Both also have numerous independent editorial projects and books to their credit. Herbert Katz is now vice-president and editor of M. Evans and Company.

The Katzes, with their two children, live in Manhattan, where their interest in museums continues to grow.